A PINCH OF
HERBS

A PINCH OF
HERBS

Herbs for Beauty, Health & Cooking
Recipes & Traditions

KATY HOLDER & GAIL DUFF

CHARTWELL
BOOKS, INC.

A QUARTO BOOK

Published by Chartwell Books
A Division of Book Sales, Inc.
114 Northfield Avenue
Edison, New Jersey 08837

This edition produced for sale in the U.S.A., its territories
and dependencies only.

ISBN 0-7858-0666-0

This book was designed and produced by
Quarto Publishing plc
The Old Brewery
6 Blundell Street
London N7 9BH

Senior Art Editor: Clare Baggaley
Assistant Art Editor: Sally Bond
Editor: Cathy Marriott
Copy Editors: Mary Senechal, Deborah Savage
Designer: Allan Mole
Picture Researcher: Susannah Jayes
Picture Research Manager: Giulia Hetherington
Photographer: David Sherwin
Photographer's Assistant: Lee Patterson
Stylist: Maureen Kane
Illustrators: Jane Smith, Elisabeth Dowle
Art Director: Moira Clinch
Assistant Art Director: Penny Cobb
Editorial Director: Mark Dartford

Typeset in Great Britain by Central Southern Typesetters, Eastbourne
Manufactured in Hong Kong by Regent Publishing Services Ltd
Printed in China by Leefung-Asco Printers Ltd

CONTENTS

INTRODUCTION

"What is a herb?" asked Alcuin, Abbot of the monastery of St. Martin at Tours in France. And the Emperor Charlemagne, who had asked him to draw up a list of plants for the imperial gardens, replied: "A herb is the friend of physicians and the praise of cooks."

Charlemagne, the emperor of France and the Holy Roman Empire in the 8th and 9th centuries, commissioned a list of plants and herbs grown in the Imperial Gardens.

6

A herb is a plant whose leaves, flowers, and, sometimes, stems are put to a purpose that enhances our lives. Herbs are valued in the kitchen where they give a special flavor to sweet and savory dishes; they can be used in preparations to scent our bodies and our surroundings; and they can be used as natural medicines. Most herbs contain an aromatic oil, often called the essential oil, which gives them their characteristic scent, flavor, and healing properties. Another distinguishing feature is, whatever the use to which herbs are put, usually only small amounts are needed to attain the desired effect.

In years gone by, the term "herb" was applied to any green plant, including cabbages, celery, and artichokes. Today, however, we confine the name to the small, powerful plants that add zest to our lives and delight to our surroundings. They have always been loved and, although they were largely neglected in the early years of the 20th century, their properties are now even more highly valued.

In an age of canned foods, artificial flavorings, chemical cures, and even fresh-air sprays in a can, a backlash developed. We looked back to an era when life moved at a slower pace, an era of aromatic gardens, of still-rooms, of pot-herbs, of the remedies of the wise woman—and we rediscovered herbs.

The world was getting smaller as people traveled to foreign countries and brought back fresh ideas, and ethnic communities with their own cooking styles settled in this country. To reproduce newly discovered dishes, we needed the herbs to make them taste authentic. Supermarkets and farmers' markets observed the trend, and now a wide range of herbs, both fresh

A field of fragrant lavender waiting to be harvested, in Norfolk, England.

Dried herbs—including fennel, chervil, tarragon, parsley, and chives—for sale in Vaison-la-Romaine Market, Vaucluse, France.

almost intangible. In a world full of mechanical gadgets and of entertainment at the push of a button, we need an experience that we can achieve for ourselves and, in doing so, acquire a certain amount of satisfaction. Herbs can provide this. Whether you are flavoring a special dish, making a gargle to ease a sore throat, perfuming a room, or beautifying yourself with a face pack, you are creating something that will improve your life—and that is important to us all.

If you go one step farther and grow your own herbs, then you will really be able to appreciate them. By preparing the ground (or the flower-pot), sowing the seed, nurturing and planting out the seedlings, and watching them grow, you will be taking part in the natural cycle of the seasons. You can enjoy the experience, take pride in your achievement, and benefit from the results. Herbs are not just the province of physicians and cooks—they are the friend and the praise of everyone.

Fragrant herbs flourish in a south-facing walled garden. This garden has a range of herbs growing, including eau de cologne mint, lavender, comfrey, sage, rosemary, and scented geraniums.

and dried, is available to everybody. Besides using them in new-found dishes, we can explore the older recipe books and reproduce the forgotten flavors of our own past.

To maintain their health, people have also turned to herbs for gentle cures and to holistic practitioners who treat the whole person, rather than one symptom. Herbs have featured prominently in this search. Herbal medicine and its associated treatments, such as aroma-therapy, have become a respected form of healthcare; ideas from all over the world are being collected together for study, and more scientific research is being conducted into the effectiveness of herbs than ever before. The aromatic properties of herbs have long been recognized. The mere presence in a room of a sweet herbal scent, however gentle, can lift the spirits and make being in that place more pleasant. We have also become more aware of the suffering that we can cause other living creatures in the name of beauty. Herbal cosmetics are kinder to animals and to our skins than other chemical-laden cosmetics.

Culinary, medicinal, aromatic, cosmetic: these, then, are the properties of herbs. But there is something else—something that is

7

Herb-Growing Through the Ages

When herbs were first used and man was nomadic, they had to be sought in the wild whenever they were needed. At the time of the first farmers, around 6000 B.C., when people began to have permanent homes, herbs were transplanted to convenient plots near dwellings. This was the beginning of herb gardening.

The first Roman emperor, Augustus, crowned with laurel. Laurel wreaths were a Roman symbol of victory and were worn by conquering soldiers and athletes.

8

A knight, page, and squire from late medieval times when most households grew herbs.

We know the ancient Egyptians valued herbs for medicinal, culinary, and aromatic purposes. They were excellent gardeners, and plans survive of the elaborate gardens that they laid out on the banks of the Nile. Herbs and other plants were arranged in straight rows, with paths between them. There were water channels for irrigation, and a wall or fence around the whole plot.

Herbs are frequently mentioned in the Bible, and throughout the Middle East, herb gardens were usually attached to temples and to sacred groves. Details survive, inscribed on stone tablets, of the herb gardens of King Ashurbanipal of Assyria in 668 B.C. In pre-Christian Europe, herbs were also connected with religion and were grown to be used in ceremonies by the Druids and others, as well as for general every-day purposes.

The Romans used quantities of herbs; lavender and rosemary were their favorites. They learned about herb gardening from the Egyptians, and soon after their capture of Egypt began to include a *hortus* in their villa gardens. The *hortus* was an area for growing herbs and vegetables, usually in separated beds or rows. Herbs were also grown in terracotta pots, which were placed along walkways and around courtyards. The Romans took herbs to every country they conquered, so the rosemary and thyme of the hot Mediterranean regions were soon to be found growing in Britain and northern Europe.

After the fall of the Roman Empire, many herbs were lost through lack of interest in their cultivation. Others escaped from the one-time villa gardens and became naturalized in their new countries. Herbs were still used, but not on such a grand scale. It was the monks who kept the art of herb gardening alive through the Dark Ages. In Anglo-Saxon times, the monastery herb gardens were quite small. A plan drawn up by the monks of St. Gall in 19th-century Switzerland records only 16 herbs, and the 9th-century German monk Walafrid Strabo had a similar list. At this time, gardens were for use and not for beauty. All plants were grown for a purpose—and most of them were herbs.

In the more settled medieval times, the range of garden herbs was extended, partly because the Crusaders brought home new ideas and plants from the East and from the Mediterranean. Every household grew a few plants, but it was still the monks who excelled at herb gardening, and they who were called upon to tend the sick in all communities.

As early as the 14th century, however, there emerged commercial herb growers, who cultivated their plants on plots close to town centers and sold bunches of herbs from stalls or cried them in the streets. After the Black Death that devastated Europe in the 14th century, more land became available for those who had survived. Greater numbers of people became tenant farmers with enough land to set aside for wider ranges of herbs, as well as fruits and vegetables, for family use. From then on, it was the women who took charge of these plots, growing the herbs that were most suited to their family's needs.

In Tudor times, gardens gradually became larger and more people turned to gardening for pleasure. Culinary, medicinal, and aromatic herbs were important in every household, and

An aerial view of the grounds of Château Villandoi, in the Loire region of France, showing the pattern of the formal knot garden.

there were herb gardens attached to both town and country homes. Where there was no land, herbs were grown in pots.

During this period, gardens began to be designed, and the first knot gardens were devised, influenced by the patterns on Oriental carpets, which had become popular with the rich. The knots were intended to be viewed from above and were placed under the windows of the most important rooms of the house. The design was carpetlike, and every plant in it had a significance. The beds of herbs were outlined with low hedges or evergreen herbs, such as marjoram, hyssop or thyme and, later, box. Some were planted in intricate, love-knot patterns; some were simple rectangular beds.

To relieve the formality of the garden, somewhere nearby was a "wild" section, called a "wilderness garden," where herbs were grown almost at random and where their scent was released when they were trodden underfoot. Chamomile lawns, which served the same purpose, became popular in Britain during Elizabethan times.

Many herbals and gardening books were written in the period between the late 16th and early 18th centuries. At the same time, large physic gardens were established for the cultivation of medicinal herbs. Some were privately owned by herbalists and apothecaries,

But apart from the use to be made of herbs, how beautiful an old herb garden is, and how altogether lovable.

ELEANOR SINCLAIR RHODE, *A GARDEN OF HERBS*, 1920s

who grew herbs for their practices. The last such garden in London was in operation until 1828. Others, such as the Orto Botanico in Pisa and the Orto dei Semplici in Florence, were for the use of universities and other public bodies.

During the 18th century, herb gardens became less formal and, although some of the larger houses kept their knot gardens, herbs were increasingly grown in beds and borders to give the impression of random planting. This style has prevailed to the present day.

Although country people and those with big houses maintained their herb gardens throughout the 19th century, there was little room in cities for such luxuries. In many European countries, the first half of the 20th century saw a decline of interest in herbs, but a revival in the 1960s has inspired many people to begin growing them again. In the past 20 years, many new herb farms have been set up all over the world to supply individual growers with plants and seeds and the commercial world with natural ingredients for food and remedies.

Bergamot was discovered in North America in the 17th century by early settlers. It became popular in European herb gardens because of its dramatic red flowers, sweet aroma, and use as a medical herb.

HERB LORE

Many herbs have been endowed with magical properties. They have been used as protections and love charms; they have been associated with different gods and goddesses; and they have been part of the rites of birth, marriage, and death.

Some herbs have been considered sacred, a gift of the gods, such as angelica in Scandinavia and eastern Europe, and mint in France and Spain. Some of these "holy" plants were sacred to particular gods or godesses, while others were simply special. The Anglo-Saxons had nine sacred plants: fennel, mugwort, plantain, watercress, chamomile, nettle, chervil, crab apple, and atterlothe, which has never been identified in modern terms.

SOWING, PLANTING, AND HARVESTING
Herbs that are difficult to grow or take a long time to germinate generally have the most lore associated with their planting. Parsley is a notoriously slow grower, and the legend is widespread that it visits the devil nine (or sometimes seven) times before sprouting. In some parts of England, it was always planted on Good Friday to prevent the devil from getting involved and to ensure good luck and happiness for the coming year. In other countries it was considered unlucky to sow the seeds across the garden, instead of along it. "It takes an honest man to grow parsley well" is one saying. "Parsley only grows where the missus is master" is another. And in the southern states it was thought unlucky to take parsley plants to the garden of a new house.

When it comes to harvesting herbs, the recommended times to do so were once governed by the phases of the moon. Some herbs could only be cut with certain implements. It was not thought right, for example, to cut mint with iron.

PROTECTIONS
People have hung bunches of herbs on doors, over beds, and in other parts of the house to protect them against evil spirits and demons, nightmares, diseases, and the supposed effects of witchcraft. Basil was hung in Hindu households to safeguard the spirit of the family. Rosemary was a popular protection in Spanish and Italian houses, and in Spain travelers wore it in their hats to ward off evil on the road. Rosemary placed under the pillow was thought to prevent nightmares. In Britain, vervain, dill, and St. John's wort were the herbs to deter witches, but they also featured in midsummer spells. Fennel was hung on doors, stuffed into keyholes, and hung from the rafters on midsummer's eve to keep evil away.

HERBS OF THE GODS AND GODDESSES
The Greeks had many sacred plants. Bay (laurel) was dedicated to Apollo and to his son Asclepius, the god of medicine. The nymph Daphne was said to have been transformed into a bay tree to save her from the pursuit of Apollo. He made himself a bay wreath as a consolation. Menthe (mint) was another nymph, who was loved by Hades of the Underworld, and was turned into a mint plant by his wife Persephone out of jealousy.

Plantain, one of the nine sacred plants of the Anglo-Saxons.

The Holy Herbs Charm

Thyme and Fennel, two exceeding mighty ones,
These herbs the wise Lord made
Holy in the Heavens; He let them down,
Placed them, and sent them into the seven worlds
As a cure for all, the poor and the rich.

PASSED DOWN BY ORAL TRADITION. DATE AND AUTHOR UNKNOWN.

Rosemary

A sprig of it hath a dumb language that meketh it the chosen emblem of our funeral wakes and in our buriall grounds.

SIR THOMAS MORE, 16TH CENTURY

CHRISTIAN ASSOCIATIONS

There are many Christian legends surrounding rosemary. In Spain, for example, it was revered as one of the bushes that gave shelter to the holy family during their flight into Egypt. The flowers changed from white to blue when the Virgin Mary hung her cloak on a rosemary bush while she rested. Rosemary was said to grow to the same height as Christ, and after 33 years (his age when he died), the bush would become

Lovage, with its pungent, celery-scented leaves, was once worn in a small bag around the neck to attract a sweetheart.

wider but no higher. Wild thyme and fennel were other herbs associated with the Virgin Mary, and they were used together in charms.

HERBS AS SYMBOLS

The same herb sometimes represents different meanings in different places and times. In contrast to basil's high status in the Hindu world, the ancient Greeks associated it with poverty and misfortune, symbolized by a ragged woman with a pot of basil at her side. Fennel has been a symbol of flattery as well as honor; marigolds have variously stood for jealousy, constancy, and obedience; sage has been an insult; chamomile a sign of humility; and rosemary symbolized the fidelity of lovers. Fennel, thyme, and borage have endured as symbols of courage. Roman soldiers and gladiators ate fennel seeds to gain bravery; and Lancastrian ladies in England embroidered a bee hovering over wild thyme on the scarves they gave to their knights fighting the Wars of the Roses in the 15th century.

LOVE AND MARRIAGE

Many are the herbs that have been put into love charms and aphrodisiacs, and which have been carried or strewn at weddings to bring good luck and fertility. Basil has long been linked with love. In Crete it was called "love washed with tears"; and in Moldavia, it was said that a young man would fall in love with any girl from whom he accepted a sprig of basil. A favorite aphrodisiac was cilantro, alone or mixed with violets and valerian. Lovage, savory, dill, and tarragon have all been ingredients of love potions. Rosemary was a favorite wedding herb throughout Europe in the 16th and 17th centuries. Bridal pozies have included dill for luck, marigolds for constancy, and rosemary for remembrance and fidelity.

IMMORTAL HERBS

In China, it was thought that eating cilantro would make you immortal, but people in other countries were content to believe that it simply prolonged life. In the French language of flowers, rosemary represents the rekindling of lost energy. Bankes's *Herbal*, published in England in 1525, says: "Make thee a box of the wood of Rosemary and smell to it and it shall preserve thy youth." The Laplanders looked to their sacred herb angelica to prolong life, chewing and smoking it like tobacco.

GROWING HERBS

*F*OR A CONSTANT SUPPLY OF GOOD-QUALITY, FRESH HERBS, THERE IS NO BETTER WAY THAN GROWING

THEM YOURSELF. *M*OST HERBS FLOURISH IN A LIGHT, WELL-DRAINED SOIL.

*H*erbs are simple to cultivate: they establish themselves easily, grow quickly, and need little attention. Large amounts of space are not necessary: herbs will flourish in a small, sunny corner of the garden; in tubs and pots on the patio; in windowboxes or hanging baskets; and in small pots on the kitchen windowsill.

FINDING AND PREPARING AN OUTDOOR LOCATION
Before you choose your herbs, decide where your herb garden is going to be and how you

*P*ots of low-growing, bushy herbs, such as lemon thyme, look attractive when placed along the edges of paths.

*S*tunning displays can be achieved by placing pots of herbs within a design of herb beds and borders. Here, lemon balm forms the feature in this patio-style herb garden.

will design it. Decide which herbs you are going to grow and how you will arrange them.

It is probable that your range of herbs will have originated from more than one country and even from more than one type of habitat. You, therefore, have to find a soil and site that are a good compromise, in which all the herbs will flourish.

Most herbs enjoy a light, dry, well-drained soil. The ideal site is within easy reach of the house, in a sheltered and sunny spot—preferably south facing. A little shade on one side will help plants such as woodruff which do not like the full sun. Alternatively, you can create a shady patch nearby by arranging piles of brushwood around the area or by sticking twigs in the ground to make a "fence."

There are also herbs, such as valerian and bergamot, which prefer damp growing conditions. If you have space, create an artificially damp area by burying a perforated sheet of plastic 12 to 18 inches under the surface and watering regularly.

Soil for herb-growing should be enriched with organic compost or well-rotted farmyard manure, or with a commercial organic product. Use a combination recommended for herb-growing by the manufacturers. If soil is acid, add a little lime.

OTHER PLACES TO GROW HERBS

RAISED BEDS

If you have a small garden, a raised bed makes an ideal feature. Old bricks, local stone, even logs can be used to make the walls of the bed. Line the bottom with stones or rubble to allow good drainage, and fill the bed with three parts top-soil to which you have added two parts peat and one-and-a-half parts fine gravel or gritty sand.

Trailing plants are ideal to soften the edges of raised beds. Build up the height of the plants toward the back, if the bed is against a wall, or in the middle, if the bed is free-standing.

ROCK GARDENS AND SLOPING GARDENS

You can build rock gardens and sloping gardens on naturally occurring slopes, or you can build them up artificially with a layer of rubble, one of gravel, and finally top-soil as for raised beds.

GRAVEL PATHS

Herbs originating from dry countries, such as lavender, and thyme, flourish on gravel paths. To keep the plants healthy, the path needs careful preparation. Dig it out to a depth of 12

A herb garden should be essentially a garden enclosed; a sanctuary of sweet and placid pleasure; a garden of peace and of sweet scents.

ELEANOR SINCLAIR RHODE, *A GARDEN OF HERBS*, 1920S

inches and half fill it with rubble. Cover this with upturned slices of turf (cut from the ground), about 4 inches thick and measuring approximately 12 x 18 inches, to provide moisture and soil. Finally, add a covering layer of gravel.

CHOOSING YOUR HERBS

A good way to choose the herbs that will best suit your needs and your plot is to obtain some catalogs from herb farms. These usually contain all the information you will need, such as main uses (culinary, aromatic, or medicinal), how the herbs grow (annual, biennial, or perennial), preferred growing location and soil type, and height of the fully grown plants. They will also say whether you can buy seeds, plants, or both.

A 17th-century herb garden, enclosed within railings and consisting of raised beds of varying shapes.

13

Herbs always look attractive against a background of gravel. These are grown in a brick-enclosed circle in the gravel path.

14

GROWING HERBS IN TUBS AND POTS

Herbs can be grown in tubs, pots, window-boxes, and half barrels of countless shapes and sizes. To prepare the containers, cover the bottom with stones or pieces of broken terra-cotta pots. If the tubs are large, line them with upturned slices of turf. Cover these with a mixture of soil and shingle, and add 10 parts fresh loam mixed with one part lime and bonemeal, mixed together. Tubs should be filled to within 2 inches of the top.

To keep herbs indoors, choose pots to fit a sunny windowsill. Put a stone into the bottom of each pot and fill with a soil-based potting medium. Place the pots in small trays. Water the herbs from the bottom, letting them dry out completely between waterings. Feed them regularly during the growing season.

GROWING HERBS FROM SEED

If you want more than two of each plant, it is most economical to grow herbs from seed. For plants to be ready in the spring, sow your seeds indoors in the fall. Have a different seed tray for each herb and fill it with a medium loam gritty soil potting medium, which gives good drainage and aeration. Sprinkle the seeds over, making sure they are spaced out, then cover them with a little more compost. Water the seeds very lightly, cover the tray with a sheet of glass or clear plastic, and put it in a warm place, out of direct sunlight, until the seeds

begin to germinate. Keep the compost damp.

When the first seedlings appear, remove the cover and put the tray into brighter light. Water them regularly. When the seedlings are about 1½ inches tall, transfer them to small pots filled with fresh potting soil. In the spring, harden the plants off by putting them outside during the day and bringing them in at night. After two weeks, they should be ready for planting out.

Most annual and perennial seeds can be planted outdoors in the spring, and biennial seeds in the autumn. After the seeds have germinated, thin them out if necessary, or wait until they have grown more sturdy and transplant them.

OTHER MEANS OF PROPAGATION

CUTTINGS

This method is ideal for the shrubby herbs, such as rosemary, thyme, sage, hyssop, and lavender. Cut a short piece of stem (about (3 inches long) from the main plant, just below a leaf joint. Put the cutting into a potting medium in a small pot, water it lightly, and cover it with a jar for a week to keep it humid. Remove the jar and leave the cutting to grow to about twice its original size before planting out. (Each herb will take a different length of time.) Some cuttings, such as those from mint and rosemary, will root if they are simply put into a

Even if you have only a small space you can still grow herbs successfully. A parsley pot, for example, can overflow with a wide selection of herbs.

jar of water. Transfer them to a pot as soon as the roots develop.

Root cuttings

With plants that spread by means of runners, such as mint, take off a section of the horizontal root that has a stem growing from it. Put it into a potting medium and keep it humid for the first week. Keep the plant in the pot for four more weeks, ensuring the potting medium stays moist, before planting out.

Root division

This is suitable for perennial plants more than two years old. Dig them up and either pull the roots apart or cut them with a knife. When you are dealing with plants that have large, spreading roots, such as sorrel, cut the roots crosswise into short pieces with a knife. Plant them into the ground where you want them to grow.

A wheel-shaped bed makes an attractive and easy-to-tend herb plot. This one has been newly planted.

These herbs have been grown in strips in the compartments of a plastic container and are now ready for either repotting, or planting out, in the garden.

15

PRESERVING HERBS

If you grow more fresh herbs than you can use, the answer is to preserve some

for using during the winter.

The characteristic scents and flavors of herbs are produced by the essential oils of the plants. To maintain the aroma and the taste, these essential oils must be preserved after careful gathering.

HARVESTING

The greatest amount of oil is produced just before the plant flowers, so this is the best time to harvest herbs for preserving. Choose a dry, warm day, after the dew has dried but before the sun becomes really hot. Cut the herbs with sharp scissors or secateurs and handle the sprigs carefully. You can safely cut away about one-third of perennial herbs, shaping the plants as you do so. Annual plants can be cut to a height of about 4 inches. Taking out their middle spike will encourage side shoots to grow. Cut only as many herbs as you can process in one day, and take them indoors, out of the sunlight, as soon as possible. Discard any damaged or diseased twigs or leaves.

DRYING HERBS

Herbs can be dried in bunches or on racks. They shrink as they dry, so tie bunches with strips of stretchy fabric, such as old pairs of thick tights, cut about 1 inch wide, because the dried herbs will fall out of string ties. Make a loop for hanging in one end of the strip, and cut a slit in the other end. Pass the strip once around approximately six herb sprigs. Put the looped end through the slit and pull the strip tight before hanging up. As the herbs

During harvesting in Provence, lavender is often tied in bunches. Afterward, the bunches are left to dry in a cool, airy place.

16

dry, the tie will tighten to keep them secure.

Hang your bunches of herbs in a warm, dry, airy room or out-building, away from steam and excessive heat. The temperature should not exceed 90°F.

If you intend to dry herbs frequently, it will be useful to construct drying racks. Make rectangular frames of light wood, strengthened with diagonal crosspieces, and cover them with cheesecloth. Place the racks side by side, or they can be designed so they stack. If you are adding herbs to the rack over a period of time, always put the freshest on the top rack, so the moisture evaporates and rises from them freely and is not absorbed by other plants.

In ideal conditions, herbs will dry in four or five days. They should remain a bright, fresh color, the stems should snap easily, and the leaves should be crisp.

DRYING HERBS IN A MICROWAVE OVEN

To dry herbs in a microwave oven, chop them finely and spread them out on a double layer of paper towels. Microwave them on High for 1½ minutes. The more delicate herbs may be quite dry by this time, while others should be stirred around and microwaved for one minute longer. Check them once more, and stir and microwave again if necessary until the herbs are dry, crisp, and bright green.

STORING DRIED HERBS

Strip the leaves carefully from the stems and leave them whole. This will preserve more flavor than crumbling them.

Store dried herbs in airtight and lightproof containers, such as wood, earthenware, or metal canisters, or jars with dark-colored glass. Place them in a cool place. They will keep their flavor for about six months. Unused herbs, which will lose some of their flavor, can be sprinkled over pot plants' soil to keep away insects.

FREEZING HERBS

Large leaves, such as those of mint or basil, can be stripped from the stems, frozen separately on trays, and stored in the freezer in sealed plastic bags for up to six months. There is no need to blanch them first. To use, crumble them into cooked dishes. The small leaves of thyme can be treated in the same way.

Large bunches of parsley and herbs of a similar texture, such as chervil, can be finely chopped before freezing in sealed bags for up to four months. To use, take them out by the spoonful. Remember to reseal the bag.

The more delicate herbs, such as dill and fennel, can be chopped and frozen in ice cubes. Three-quarters fill ice-cube trays with the chopped herbs, top up with water, and freeze. Store the ice cubes in sealed plastic bags for up to four months. Add the ice cubes to dishes at the beginning of their cooking time.

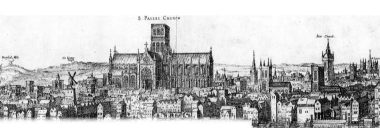

Here's fine rosemary, sage and thyme.
Come, buy my ground ivy.
Here's featherfew, gillyflowers and rue.
Come, buy my knotted marjoram too!
Here's fine lavender for your clothes,
Here's parsley and winter savory,
And heartsease which all do choose.
Here's balm and hyssop and cinquefoil,
All fine herbs it is well known.
Let none despise the merry, merry cries
Of famous London town.

ROXBURGH BALLADS, 18TH CENTURY

MEDICAL HERBALISM

MEDICAL HERBALISM IS THE MEDICINAL USE OF PLANTS. IT HAS BEEN PRACTICED FOR AT LEAST

4 MILLION YEARS—AS LONG AS HUMAN BEINGS HAVE BEEN EATING PLANT-BASED FOODS.

A woodcut of a Chinese doctor from the 1850s. The artist wrote, "These doctors always feel the pulses of both wrists. Their medicines consist mostly of herbs."

The first medicinal herbs were probably chosen by instinct and possibly also by a method related to that used to dowse for water. It is interesting to note that the same plants were chosen in many widely separated countries that had no known contact with one another. Treatments are likely to have been discovered on the principle that the craving for certain foods indicated the body's need for them at the time. For example, the strong-flavored bitter herbs, such as dandelion and sorrel, were sought out in the spring. We know that these plants contain vitamin C and therefore prevent scurvy—a likely springtime ailment after a limited winter diet. Early healers simply knew that those plants kept the body healthy.

As human groups became more settled, medicine became more established. With the advance of cultures came written records of herbs and remedies. In 2800 B.C., the Chinese

Many common herbs that are best known for their culinary properties also make effective home remedies.

herbalist Shen Nung compiled a list of 366 medicinal herbs, many of which are still used. The ancient Egyptians grew and imported medicinal herbs, which were administered by recognized doctors and by the growers

In ancient Greece, people who grew and supplied herbs were called *rhizotomoki* (root-gatherers), and the earliest Greek herbal, written by Diocles of Carystius in 4 B.C., was called *Rhizotomika*. The famous herbal of the Greek physician Dioscorides, published in the 1st century A.D., had a profound influence on both Greek and Roman medicine. Armed with its knowledge, physicians followed the Roman legions throughout the Empire, taking their plants with them.

The leading 2nd-century physician Galen, doctor to the Roman emperors, had an influence on medicine that lasted for 1,500 years. Some of his remedies were highly complex, and from his time onward a distinction was made between the doctor, who prescribed expensive formulas, and the healer, who used a "specific," a particular herb for one particular effect.

After the Romans, the monks carried on the medical tradition, and there was much interaction between the monasteries of Europe, with monks of all countries exchanging ideas, remedies, and plants. In England, herbal learning was greatly advanced by the later Anglo-Saxons, and in Italy in the 10th century, a medical school based on medical herbalism was founded at Salerno.

Plant cures also featured prominently in Arab medicine, and from the Middle Eastern writer Ibn Said (called Avicenna in the West) came the idea of linking herbal plants with astrology. He believed that each herb was under the influence of or governed by a particular planet.

In early medieval times, both Arab and European medicine became even more complex. Physicians to the rich included pounded gemstones in their remedies in a bid to convince the public that medicines must consist of many expensive ingredients to work. Medieval

The apothecary diagnosed and treated patients. His cures were based mainly on herbs.

physicians also adopted such practices as bleeding and blistering, which were not abandoned until the middle of the 19th century.

This was the beginning of a medical profession based on expensive chemical cures which, in those early years, probably killed more people than they cured. Ordinary people, however, could not afford physicians. They relied on their own knowledge and the skills of local healers to dispense herbal remedies. Many people grew their own herbs and knew where to find them in the hedgerows, and it was often the duty of the clergyman's wife or the lady of the manor to look after the health of the village. During the 16th and 17th centuries, herbals, such as that of Nicholas Culpeper, were published to help.

The first European settlers in the New World took their plant remedies with them. In the early years they also acquired a little knowledge about local plants from the native Americans. In the pioneer settlements, home ministering of herbal medicine was much as it had been in Europe.

As they were newly settled, the colonies were open to fresh ideas, and several herbal practitioners, including Samuel Thomson and Wooster Beach, enjoyed recognition and success during the 19th century. Homeopathy

was founded in Germany by Samuel Hahnemann, and the first homeopathy clinic in the United States was opened in New York City in 1825 and proved popular.

In Britain and the rest of Europe, however, most people were turning toward the chemical remedies which were being newly marketed for home treatments. These included previously popular calomel (mercurous chloride), along with plant-based drugs, such as laudanum (a tincture of opium), and purges, such as senna and rhubarb. The plants were used singly, in large quantities, and only to sedate and purge. This is not like gentle herbal medicine, which uses relatively small amounts of many different herbs. The seeds of chemical medicine had been sown, and for the first half of the 20th century, medical herbalists struggled for recognition.

In the 1960s, however, the chemical bubble began to burst when fears of side effects spread. In 1977 the World Health Organization started to advocate the use of traditional herbal medicines around the world, and since then much research has been done into the true benefits of medicinal herbs.

Many people have realized, for simple common ailments, they can treat themselves with a herbal infusion rather than resorting to expensive chemical pills. With a little herbal knowledge, we can all be our own doctors of physic using plants from our own gardens.

19

In the 15th century, the rich were able to buy expensive and sometimes chemical-based remedies. The poor had to make do with home treatment using their own herbs.

Herbal Treatments in the Home

Herbal remedies, such as those to ease a common cold or sore throat, are very easy to make and can work quickly. Other herbal treatments function slowly and steadily.

For common ailments, simple herbal remedies are ideal. Side effects are few, but those who suffer from a long-term illness, such as a heart complaint, or women who are pregnant should only use herbal treatments under the advice and guidance of a doctor. For serious or persistent illness you should always consult your family doctor first. With your doctor's approval you should then consult a recommended medical herbalist. There are also many in-depth medical herbals available, which have been written for home use and they should be consulted before any self-treatment.

Buying Herbs for Home Treatment

Always use the highest-quality herbs available. Organically grown herbs from your own herb garden, either fresh or dried, are the best. Alternatively, buy dried herbs from respected suppliers of herbs for medical use. Many of them sell by mail order. Purchase only as much as you need for your course of treatment. Do not keep dried herbs for longer than six months.

Herbal Preparations

Infusion
Put the chopped fresh or dried herb into a container, pour boiling water over, cover, and leave for the length of time specified in the remedy. Strain and reserve the liquid.

Decoction
Put the chopped fresh or dried herb into an enamel or stainless-steel saucepan with the amount of water specified in the remedy. Then cover and boil for the time stated in the recipe. Strain and reserve the liquid.

Fragrant, culinary, and medicinal herbs can be grown in separate areas of the herb garden, although many have dual uses.

Compress
Moisten a clean piece of lint in an infusion or decoction and apply it to the affected area. Compresses can be used for bruises, sprains, and inflamed areas. If they are required only for a short time, for example up to 15 minutes, they can be held on the affected part by hand; if longer, secure with bandages.

Poultice
Use dried and powdered herbs or roots, such as comfrey or marshmallow root. Mix 1 tablespoon of the powder with a little hot water or hot comfrey infusion to make a paste. Sandwich the hot paste between two pieces of sterile lint and apply it to the affected area .

Tisane
A tisane is an alternative name for an infusion. There is no standard recipe.

Herbal oil
The chopped herb or herb sprigs are put into a screw-top jar or a bottle of oil and covered. The oil is left in a warm place for up to three weeks depending on the recipe and agitated frequently. It is then strained and stored in a clean jar or bottle.

A herbal infusion is made just like tea, by pouring boiling water over fresh or dried herbs.

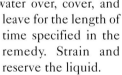

A SELECTION OF HERBAL REMEDIES

Dried herbs are used for all but one of these remedies. Double the amounts for fresh herbs.

Relief for a Common Cold

There is no cure for a common cold; it has to take its course. But this infusion will bring considerable relief.

2 tbsp dried yarrow
2 tbsp dried elderflowers
1 tbsp dried peppermint
Small pinch cayenne pepper
Honey for sweetening (optional)

Put the dried herbs and cayenne pepper into a teapot. Pour in 2½ cups boiling water. Cover and leave to stand for 5 minutes. Strain and drink hot or warm, over the period of one hour, adding honey to taste if required. This may be repeated twice more during the day.

Remedy for an Upset Stomach

This infusion should settle a stomach that feels queasy, such as a bout of travel sickness. It will also help to calm the stomach after vomiting.

1 tbsp dried peppermint
¼ tsp fennel seeds

Put the peppermint and fennel seeds into a pitcher or small teapot. Pour in 1¼ cups boiling water. Cover and leave for 10 minutes. Strain and sip while it is warm.

A Tisane for Sleeplessness

Herbs are gentle sleep inducers. They help you to relax but do not leave you groggy in the morning.

1 tsp dried chamomile
1 tsp dried lime (linden) flowers
1 dried hop flower
Honey for sweetening

Put the chamomile, lime flowers, and hop flower into a pitcher or small teapot. Pour in 1¼ cups boiling water. Cover and leave to infuse for 10 minutes. Strain and sweeten to taste with honey. Relax and sip the tisane slowly.

An Oil for Athlete's Foot

Use a good-quality oil for this; jojoba or wheatgerm oil can be substituted for almond oil. If these are unavailable, choose a high-quality olive oil. The oils may be purchased from drug stores, beauty suppliers, or some herbalist suppliers. This is a remedy in which fresh herbs work better than dried.

4 tbsp almond oil
1 tbsp chopped fresh thyme leaves

Pour the oil into a small, clear glass container. Add the thyme and cover tightly. Leave the container on a sunny windowsill or in a warm place for one week, shaking every 48 hours. Strain. Apply to the affected area night and morning.
If the remedy is for immediate use, put the oil and the thyme into a small saucepan. Heat them very gently, without letting the oil bubble, for 30 minutes. Strain and cool before using.

A Compress for Bruises

Comfrey is a well-known aid to the fast healing of bruises, sprains, and breaks.

2 tbsp dried comfrey
Piece of lint large enough to cover the affected area

Put the comfrey and 2½ cups water into a stainless-steel or enamel saucepan. Bring them gently to a boil. Reduce the heat, cover, and boil for 30 minutes. Strain.
Soak the piece of lint in the decoction, wring it out and apply it, as hot as possible without burning, to the affected area.

A Warm Mouthwash to Ease Toothache

This infusion will ease the pain of toothache, but will not get rid of the cause. It is best to consult a dentist as soon as possible.

1 tsp dried red sage (or common sage if red is unavailable)
1 clove

Put the sage and clove into a pitcher. Pour in 1¾ cups boiling water. Cover and leave until it is warm. Strain and use as a mouthwash immediately. Any remaining mouthwash can be kept covered in the refrigerator for up to two days.

21

Aromatic Herbs

The scents of herbs can be refreshing, relaxing, healing, and sensuous. Sitting or walking in a fragrant herb garden can ease stressed minds, and herbal scents have long been used to combat disease, repel insects, and even supposedly keep away evil spirits.

The Romans scented their baths with herbal extracts and used herbal oils for perfumes and massages.

22

A 15th-century German woodcut showing a wattle garden with roses.

If a room is pervaded with an underlying sweet scent of herbs it improves everyone's well-being. The ancient Egyptians were the first to show interest in the aromatic properties of herbs. They made scented ointments for their bodies and created potpourris by burying large crocks of scented rose petals in the ground to assist fermentation. There are frequent mentions of herbs in both the Bible and the Koran; the Song of Songs gives thanks for "all things good, even pleasant smells for our noses."

The Greeks planted fragrant herb gardens around their houses, believing that the sweet sharp scents would keep the household healthy. The Romans hung up bunches of herbs to deter insects, scattered rose petals over banqueting floors, and scented their communal baths with rosemary. All manner of sweet-smelling herbs were planted in symbolic patterns in Arab gardens of the early medieval period, to be used for perfuming the body and surrounding environment. The Crusaders learned from the Arabs and returned to England with ideas for fragrant gardens, perfumes, and for scenting houses. The custom began of strewing the floors of churches and living rooms with aromatic herbs which gave out their scent as they were crushed underfoot.

It was in the 16th-century that the use of fragrant herbs in the home became really popular throughout Europe. Larger houses had a stillroom, where women made potpourris, pomanders, and sweet bags for linen, and where they distilled the essence of flowers and herbs for perfumes and washing waters. Those without any space for a stillroom worked at the kitchen table. Scented herbal preparations became essential deodorizers in houses with small, high windows, beaten mud floors, and no protection from damp.

The art of the stillroom was taken to the United States and employed as soon as settlements became established and peaceful. It began to die out in the 19th century in countries such as Britain when industrialization caused populations to move to towns; but in country districts it remained popular until the beginning of the 20th century. It never entirely disappeared, however, and there is now a revival of interest. You can buy potpourri and natural fragrances; and with a selection of scented herbs and a few additional ingredients you can make your scented preparations.

Herbs in Pots and Bunches

Bringing a pot containing a fragrant herb, such as rosemary, into the house is the simplest way of scenting a room, and was often recommended in the 16th century.

Hanging up a bunch of herbs was a Roman idea which can easily be employed today. This not only scents the room but can also keep away insects. Use the following herbs singly or in any mixtures that please you:

To freshen the air: lavender, rosemary, santolina (cotton lavender), hyssop, mint, thyme, woodruff.

To cool the air: lavender, rosemary, wormwood, woodruff.

To deter flies: rue, tansy, pennyroyal, peppermint, basil.

Potpourri

A potpourri is a fragrant mixture of dried herbs and flowers which is kept in a perforated container or open bowl in a place where its scent can perfume a room.

The original method of making a potpourri, devised by the ancient Egyptians, was to bury a crock of sweet-scented leaves and petals in the ground until the contents fermented and became a dry, highly aromatic mixture. This technique gave potpourri its name which, translated literally from the French, means "rotten pot." It was employed by the Greeks, Romans, and Arabs, and was the method used in 16th-century stillrooms.

This traditional way of making potpourri is known today as the "moist" method. It takes a long time and you need a great many fresh flowers, but the result is a mixture with a strong, sweet fragrance that will last for at least five years.

The "dry" method of making potpourri is much simpler, and this is the best means to choose if you have more aromatic herbs than flowers. You can grow herbs especially for a dry potpourri, and you can also use a large proportion of culinary herbs. Many herbs have to be cut back in the summer, and it would be impossible to use them all in the kitchen, so making a potpourri is an excellent means of ensuring they are not wasted. All herbs and flowers for a dry pot-pourri should be dried until they are crisp. If you are unable to grow your own herbs and flowers, many of those listed below can be bought dried from herbalists.

HERBS FOR DRY POTPOURRI: Agrimony, balm, bay, clary sage, costmary, leaves of scented geraniums (such as mint or lemon), lavender, lemon verbena, marjoram, mints of various sorts (eau de Cologne mint, apple mint, spearmint, bergamot mint), pennyroyal, pineapple sage, southernwood, tansy, thyme (common and other fragrant thymes), woodruff, wormwood.

FLOWERS FOR DRY POTPOURRI: Rose petals, carnations, honeysuckle, heliotrope, jasmin, orange blossom, peony, stocks, violets, wallflowers. You can also add some flowers purely for their color, such as cornflower, hibiscus, larkspur, marigolds, nasturtiums, salvia, and zinnias.

OTHER INGREDIENTS: These include spices, woods, and the dried peels of citrus fruits, which are added in small quantities. Spices are best bought whole and crushed with a mortar and pestle just before you add them.

FIXATIVES: These help to preserve the scent of a potpourri. Orrisroot powder is the most popular and readily available. It is the dried, ground root of *Iris florentina*; *I. germanica*, or *I. pallida*.

ESSENTIAL OILS: These heighten the scent of a dry potpourri. Choose oils that match your herbs (for example, use lavender oil if there is a large proportion of lavender in the mixture), and add only a drop at a time, because you will need very little. Essential oils for potpourri can be bought from herbalists, drug stores, and health-food stores.

Hanged up in houses, it [woodruff] doth very well attemper the aire, coole and make fresh the place to the delight and comfort of such as are therein.

JOHN GERARD, 1596

Herbal Potpourri

This is a potpourri with a fresh, clean scent, made with a selection of fragrant herbs that are common in most herb gardens.

1½ oz dried lavender flowers
1 oz hyssop
1 oz marjoram or oregano leaves
½ oz thyme leaves
½ oz eau de Cologne mint or peppermint
Cinnamon sticks together measuring 10 inches
½ nutmeg, freshly grated
2 tbsp orrisroot powder
4 drops lavender oil

Leave all the herbs to dry until crisp. Mix the dried herbs together in a bowl. Crush the cinnamon sticks with a mortar and pestle or grind them between 2 sheets of waxed paper with a rolling pin. Add them to the herbs. Add the nutmeg and orrisroot powder and mix well. Add the lavender oil, stirring after each drop. Put the potpourri in a plastic bag, seal, and leave for one month. Transfer it to a jar or bowl for display.

BASIC METHOD: Select the herbs and flowers that will determine the basic scent of the potpourri, then choose others to complement them. Mix them together and sniff. Add spices and woods to balance the overall effect. Mix again. Add essential oil, one drop at a time, mixing and testing the scent after each addition. Put the finished potpourri into a plastic bag and seal. Leave it for one month to let the fragrance blend and mature.

CONTAINERS FOR POT-POURRI: A potpourri in an open bowl will scent the room strongly for about a month, after which the scent will diminish. If you keep it in a covered bowl and remove the cover only when needed, the scent will last longer. Whichever container you choose, stir the potpourri once a day to release the scent and to prevent the top layer from losing its smell completely.

A 19th-century advertisement for James Floris, a London perfumer, who sold herbal aromatic vinegars and perfumes.

24

SWEET BAGS

Sweet bags are fabric sachets containing dried herb mixtures, which can be placed with hanging clothes or in a cupboard drawer, on a dressing table, or hung from a chair. Lavender has always been the favorite herb for sweet bags because of its fresh, clean scent and its ability to repel moths. Other moth deterring herbs are rosemary, thyme, woodruff, southern-wood and wormwood. Use them singly or mixed, and add 1 teaspoon of orrisroot powder for every 1 ounce of dried herbs. Crushed cloves or cinnamon, or small pieces of nutmeg can also be added. Choose a natural-fiber material, such as cotton, silk, or linen, with a fairly tight weave for making sweet bags. Decorate the bags with frills, ribbons, or lace and sew on loops for hanging.

As a guide, 1 ounce herb mixture will fill a rectangular bag that measures approximately 4 by 6 inches.

BURNING PERFUMES

The word perfume comes from the Latin *per* ("through") and *fumare* ("to smoke"), so to perfume a room in Roman times was to refresh it with pleasantly scented smoke. The simplest way of doing this, and probably the oldest, is to place fragrant herb sprigs on the embers of a fire. Lavender, rosemary, southernwood, and bay leaves are the most suitable.

From the 11th to the 18th century in Europe, when rush mats and beds harbored fleas, burning wormwood and rue in the room was found to be an effective and aromatic repellent. American Indians burned bunches of herbs, known as smudge sticks, for rituals and for

. . . in summer, the chimney fireplace be trimmed with a bank of fresh moss and at either end have a rosemary pot.

SIR HUGH PLATT, *DELIGHTS FOR LADIES*, 1594

Lemon and Lavender Sweet Bag Mixture

This has a fresh, clean scent and is suitable for putting in a drawer among clothes, or hanging in a closet. Orrisroot powder is the powdered root of one of three specific European irises. It is available from herbalists.

1 oz lemon verbena
1 oz lavender
1 oz hyssop
(if available)
1 tsp grated
nutmeg
1 tbsp dried
orrisroot
powder

purification, and these can also be used in the home. The herbs, often a variety of different sages, are bound tightly together to form a candle shape. When lit, they smoulder gently, emitting a pleasant scent. They can be extinguished in water, then dried and relit when needed. Smudge sticks, sometimes called sage brushes, are available from herbal stores.

One step on from scattering herbs on the fire was to heat them in a chafing dish, similar to a skillet, which was filled with sweet-smelling herbs and spices and set over hot coals. Keep an old skillet for this purpose and heat the herbs on the stovetop over low heat. It is an excellent way to get rid of cooking smells.

Queen Anne's Chafing Dish

6 tbsp rose-water
2 tsp fresh rosemary leaves
2 cloves
½ tsp sugar

Put all the ingredients into a small skillet and simmer them over low heat until the liquid has almost evaporated. Do not let the liquid boil away completely or the pan will burn.

ANNE.

Herb Candles

This is a basic method for making 2 scant cups of herb-scented wax. The specialist equipment and ingredients can be bought from candlemakers' suppliers.

EQUIPMENT
Sunflower oil for greasing molds
One or more plastic, glass, or metal molds, together totalling the volume given (herbs may damage rubber molds)
Wicking needle
Wick (use a thicker wick for wider candles)
Mold seal
Toothpicks
Double boiler or a heatproof bowl to stand in a saucepan of water
An old small saucepan
Thermometer (ordinary or specialist candle-making one)

INGREDIENTS
12 oz paraffin wax
1¼ oz stearin
⅛ tsp finely grated dye disk (green, blue, purple, or whatever color suits your herb, optional)
1 oz dried herbs, such as lavender, rosemary, thyme, or hyssop

METHOD
Lightly grease the molds. Using the wicking needle, pull the wick through the hole in the top of the mold: the length of wick used will depend on the size of mold used. Secure the wick with mold seal at the top end. Tie it to a toothpick at the other end, so it stays taut through the mold. Place the molds upside-down in a holder. (Molds often come with their own holder, or you can improvize with another container suitable for the size and shape of the mold. Thin candles can be stuck into plasticine.)

Melt the wax in a double boiler and heat gently to a temperature of 185°F. Melt the stearin and grated dye disk in a small saucepan. Add them to the wax. Stir in the herbs.

Pour the mixture into the molds, distributing the herbs evenly between them. Leave the wax for 10 minutes.

If depressions appear in the surface, top up with any remaining wax in the saucepan. Leave for 5 hours, or until the candles are set.

To remove the candles from the molds, pull gently on the toothpick, using it as a lever. If the candles appear to be stuck (the presence of herbs in the wax sometimes has this effect), dip the molds briefly into hot water.

Trim the wicks.

NOTE: The herbs will probably not remain evenly distributed throughout the candles. Some sink to the bottom, others float in the wax. This does not detract from the finished appearance.

Herb directory

Allium sativum (*Garlic*)

Garlic is a perennial plant with a flattened round bulb, made up of eight to ten sections called cloves, held together by a thin papery covering. The cloves have a savory, pungent flavor. Culinary, medicinal, cosmetic.

Allium schoenoprasum (*Chives*)

Chives are a relative of the onion. They are perennial plants which produce thin, hollow leaves from March through October. They have a mild onion flavor. Culinary.

Anethum graveolens (*Dill*)

Dill is an annual plant which has delicate feathery leaves and a rich flavor. In temperate climates it can be picked throughout the summer. The seeds are also used. Culinary, medicinal.

Artemisia dracunculus (*Tarragon*)

Tarragon is a perennial plant which dies back completely in winter and which can be picked from late spring until early fall. Its flavor is warming, spicy, and slightly sweet. Culinary, medicinal.

Borago officinalis (*Borage*)

Borage is a tall perennial plant which has large, hairy leaves and small blue and black flowers that can be picked from early summer to early fall. It has a cucumberlike flavor. Both its leaves and flowers are used. Culinary, medicinal.

Chaerophyllum sativum (*Chervil*)

Chervil is an annual from the same family as parsley, and has delicate, deeply cut leaves. Its flavor contains a hint of licorice. It can be cut in the spring, and again in the early fall and after summer seeding. Culinary, medicinal.

Coriandrum sativum (*Coriander/Cilantro*)

Coriander, or cilantro, is another relative of parsley. It is an annual, with flat, wide, toothed leaves. It has a pungent flavor. The seeds are also used. Culinary, medicinal, cosmetic.

Eruca sativa (*Arugula*)

Arugula is a perennial plant which grows in long, leafy stems. It has a slightly hot, peppery flavor. Culinary.

Foeniculum vulgare (*Fennel*)

Fennel is a tall, perennial plant with large, feathery leaves, which gradually fall backward as they grow. Its flavor is reminiscent of aniseed. The seeds are also used. Culinary, medicinal.

Laurus nobilis (*Bay*)

The bay is an evergreen tree which flourishes in tubs and in sheltered areas. The leaves, which are the part used, are of a pointed oval shape and shiny on the top. Bay has a slightly bitter, savory flavor. Culinary, medicinal, aromatic.

Lavandula vera (*Lavender*)

Lavender is a low, shrubby bush, with narrow, pointed, gray-green leaves and spikes of purple flowers. It has a sweet, sharp, pungent flavor. Culinary, medicinal, aromatic, cosmetic.

Levisticum officinale (*Lovage*)

Lovage is a tall, perennial plant, which has large, serrated leaves. The leaves can be picked throughout the summer. Its flavor is reminiscent of hot, spicy celery. Culinary, medicinal.

Melissa officinalis (*Balm*)

Balm is a bushy, perennial plant, which has heart-shaped leaves growing on long spikes, topped with whorls of small white flowers. The leaves can be picked from late spring to early fall. The flavor

is a combination of spice, honey, and lemon. Culinary, medicinal, aromatic, cosmetic.

MENTHA SPICATA (SPEARMINT)

There are many varieties of mint, the most common being *M. spicata*, or spearmint. All mints are perennial plants which spread rapidly. The oval, pointed leaves have a refreshing flavor and can be picked throughout the summer. Culinary, medicinal, cosmetic.

OCIMUM BASILICUM (BASIL)

Basil is a delicate annual plant which loves the sun and is usually harvested only in the summer months. Its bright green leaves grow from a central stem topped with spikes of white flowers. The flavor is pungent, sweet, and slightly spicy. Culinary, medicinal.

ORIGANUM MARJORANA (SWEET MARJORAM)

Sweet marjoram is one of the may varieties of marjoram. It is a perennial plant which can be picked from spring until fall. It has small, oval leaves, growing on the main and branching stems, and a savory-sweet flavor. Culinary, medicinal, aromatic.

ORIGANUM VULGARE (OREGANO OR WILD MARJORAM)

Similar in appearance and habit to sweet marjoram, oregano has a spicier flavor. Culinary.

PETROSELINUM SATIVUM (PARSLEY)

Parsley is probably the most used of all herbs. It is an annual plant with a generous supply of curled, bright-green leaves, and a mild, savory flavor. It can be picked from spring to fall. Culinary, medicinal, cosmetic.

ROSMARINUS OFFICINALIS (ROSEMARY)

Rosemary is a perennial, shrubby bush. Its small, spiked leaves, dark green on one side and gray-green on the other, can be picked throughout the year. The scent and flavor of rosemary is strong

and pungent. Culinary, medicinal, aromatic, cosmetic.

RUMEX ACETOSA (SORREL)

The garden variety of sorrel is *R. acetosa*. It is a perennial plant with large, spinachlike leaves, which are often wrinkled and tall spikes of red flowers. The leaves have a very sharp, fresh flavor, and are at their best in the spring and early summer. Culinary, medicinal.

SALVIA OFFICINALIS (SAGE)

Sage is a perennial, shrubby bush with tongue-shaped, gray-green leaves and purple flowers. It can be gathered all year but is at its best in spring and summer. The flavor is slightly spicy and savory. Culinary, medicinal.

SATUREJA MONTANA/HORTENSIS (WINTER SAVORY/SAVORY)

A small, woody, evergreen shrub, *S. montana* has little, spiky leaves and a warming, spicy flavor. *S. hortensis*, or summer savory, is a perennial, more delicate in flavor and texture. Culinary.

TARAXACUM OFFICINALE (DANDELION)

The dandelion is a wild plant which can also be cultivated. It is perennial, but its long, toothed leaves are best in spring when they are tender and delicately flavored. Culinary, medicinal, cosmetic.

THYMUS VULGARIS (GARDEN THYME)

Thyme is a low-growing perennial plant with tiny leaves and purple flowers. There are many different varieties, but *T. vulgaris* is the most widely used. Thyme has a savory-sweet flavor. Culinary, medicinal, aromatic.

URTICA DIOICA (NETTLE)

The nettle is a wild, perennial plant which grows prolifically. Its heart-shaped, serrated leaves should be picked in the spring when they are young. Nettles have a savory flavor more like a vegetable than a herb. Culinary, medicinal, cosmetic.

HERBAL BEAUTY

From earliest times, herbs have been used to enhance beauty. They are still regarded as effective cosmetics, and they are certainly the safest. Many not only contain ingredients to improve the condition of the skin and hair, but also possess attractive scents.

The first herbal cosmetics are probably as old as civilisation itself. The earliest recorded users of herbs were the ancient Egyptians, who loved to beautify themselves, coloring their hair with henna and outlining their eyes with kohl. They also knew the value of perfumes, and extracted oils from plants to make scented ointments for massaging and softening the skin.

From Roman times onward, women regarded pale-colored faces as beautiful and lightened their complexions by bathing their faces with a mixture of honey, lemon juice, and herbal infusions. A face mask to make the skin paler and soothe away wrinkles was invented in the 1st century A.D. by the Roman naturalist Pliny. It contained ground peas (or barley), egg white, honey, wine, and a secretion from narcissus bulbs. In the 17th century, Queen Henrietta Maria of England used a mixture of apricot paste and orange-flower water for the same purpose.

In 1370, Queen Elizabeth of Hungary ordered the making of a face lotion which she claimed would give the user a wrinkle-free face long into old age. The recipe, said to have been given to her by a monk, came to be called Hungary Water, and its main ingredients were rosemary and lavender. Carmelite Water,

Venus, Roman goddess of love and beauty.

Elderflower Facial Scrub

This is a very gentle exfoliant which will remove the upper layer of dead cells to leave skin feeling soft, smooth, and vibrant. It is suitable for all skin types.

1 tbsp dried elderflowers
6 tbsp boiling water
2 tbsp fine oatmeal

Put the elderflowers into a bowl or pitcher and pour the boiling water over. Cover and leave to infuse until cool, then strain. Put the oatmeal into a bowl and mix in 3 tablespoons of the elderflower infusion. Gently massage the mixture into your face for about 5 minutes. Remove the scrub with lukewarm water. Pat your face dry with a soft towel and apply a toner and moisturizer, if using.

Marjoram is one of the herbs that can be used for a scented bath. Besides adding fragrance, it can relieve aching muscles.

Hungary Water

Take to every gallon of brandy or clean Spirits, one handful of Rosemary, one handful of Lavender. I suppose the handfuls to be about a foot long a-piece; and these herbs must be cut in pieces about an Inch long. Put these to infuse in the Spirits, and with them, about one handful of Myrtle, cut as before. When this has stood three days, distil it, and you will have the finest Hungary Water that can be.

R. Bradley, *The Country Housewife and Lady's Director*, 1732

28

Fragrant chamomile has a tautening and cleansing effect on the face, and it has long been used as a rinse to bring out highlights in blonde hair.

containing balm and angelica, and first made in 1379 by nuns of the Abbey of St. Just, in France, also became popular with n o b l e - w o m e n throughout medieval Europe.

Beauty, cleanliness, and fragrance have always gone together, and the simplest cosmetics of the past were sweet washing waters. These were produced by the infusion, decoction (boiling), or distillation of sweetly scented flowers and herbs, to extract their essence. It is said that the first rosewater was made by the Arab physician Avicenna in the 10th century, but it was probably in use long before that, even though it went out of fashion in the Dark Ages. In medieval times, elaborate jars of rosewater were placed on the tables of the rich for diners to rinse their fingers and refresh their clothes. There were no forks in those days, and eating could be a messy business.

Rosewater remained popular for centuries. Waters made with rosemary, marjoram, lavender, basil, pennyroyal, and costmary were used for the same purpose; up until the 19th century, pitchers of washing water in the guest bedroom were scented with herbs.

It is also well to boil the flowers and leaves [of rosemary] in water and to wash yourself therewith every morning, omitting to dry it with a cloth, but leaving it to do so naturally. By washing thus with perseverance, the aged will retain a youthful look as long as they live.

QUOTED BY MRS. C. F. LEYEL IN *THE MAGIC OF HERBS*, 1926

Herb-scented baths had been popular with the Egyptians, Greeks, and Romans, but bathing fell out of favor after the collapse of the Roman Empire and was not a frequent occurrence again until the 17th century. Then various herbs were added to the bathwater to soften and scent the skin. In rich households, milk and oatmeal were used to increase the softening effects.

Beautiful hair has always been coveted and herbs have long been used to maintain a good head of hair. Rosemary and nettle, and chamomile and sage have been the most popular hair treatments. People have lightened their hair with chamomile and rhubarb, colored it red with henna, and darkened it with sage. These herbs are still used today.

Parsley Face Mask

Like the facial scrub, this face mask will gently exfoliate the skin, getting rid of dead skin cells and speeding up the renewal process. Parsley leaves skin feeling refreshed and is suitable for all skin types.

2 tbsp chopped fresh parsley
4 tbsp cornmeal
2–3 tbsp plain yogurt

Put the parsley and cornmeal into a bowl and mix in 2 tablespoons of the yogurt. You should be able to spread the mixture easily, so if the mask is on the dry side, add up to 1 tablespoon more of the yogurt.
Spread the mixture over your face, avoiding the area immediately around the eyes. Lie down and relax for
15 minutes.
Rinse the mask off with lukewarm water. Pat your face dry with a soft towel and then apply a toner and moisturizer, if using.

Herbal Hair Rinse

The most effective herbs for healthy, shining hair are rosemary and nettles, and both can be used as a base for rinses to revive dull hair. Rosemary is best for general use and nettles are good for hair that has dried out in the sun.

1 oz dried rosemary or fresh nettle leaves
2½ cups boiling water
Oil of lavender, lemon, or orange (for nettle leaves only)

Put the herb into a pitcher or bowl. Pour the boiling water over, cover, and leave to infuse for 2 hours. Line a strainer with cheesecloth or a coffee filter paper and strain the rinse through it. If you are using nettles, add 4 drops of your chosen oil to improve the scent, and mix well. The rinse will keep in a cool place for up to a day.
To use, wash and thoroughly rinse your hair normally. Then with your head over the sink, slowly pour the herb rinse through your hair, making sure that it reaches every part. Gently massage the rinse into your hair. Towel dry and for maximum effect leave your hair to finish drying naturally.

Herb	Effect	Skin type
Balm	Tautening	all
Chamomile	Tautening, cleansing, lightening hair color, anti-inflammatory	all
Comfrey	Softening, healing	all
Elderflower	Cleansing, lightening hair color, softening	all
Fennel	Cleansing, gentle astringent	all
Lavender	Antiseptic, stimulating	all
Lime flower	Tautening	all
Marigold	Cleansing, mildly astringent, healing	all
Mint	Strong astringent, spot cleanser	not for sensitive skins
Nettle	Cleansing, purifying, toning	all
Parsley	Cleansing, toning, helps combat thread veins	all
Rosemary	Tautening	all
Sage	Astringent, cooling	oily
Thyme	Toning, refreshing, antiseptic	all
Violet	Softening, cleansing	dry
Woodruff	For soreness from sunburn or windburn	all
Yarrow	Astringent	oily

Making Herbal Cosmetics

Herbal cosmetics are easy to make at home. The ingredients are readily available—you probably have many of them in your kitchen already. For most cosmetics, you will need only simple equipment, such as spoons, bowls, or strainers. Be sure to clean these well before and after making cosmetics. If you intend to create your own beauty treatments regularly, it is worthwhile keeping a separate set of implements just for that purpose.

Herbs to Use

The most frequently used cosmetic herbs are listed left. You can grow your own, obtain them fresh from sources that sell herbs for food, or buy them dried, direct or by mail order, from reputable herb suppliers.

Some herbs suit all skin types. Others are either astringent, which means that they have a drying effect, or emollient, which means that they contain materials that form gels when mixed with water that soften the skin. Use astringent herbs for oily skin and emollient herbs for dry skin. Other effects produced by herbs are tautening (making your skin feel smoother and tighter), and soothing or healing.

Buttermilk and Lime Flower Cleanser

This is a very gentle cleanser, suitable for all skin types. Use to cleanse the face of grime or of light makeup.

1¼ cups buttermilk
4 tbsp lime flowers
2 tbsp honey

Put the buttermilk and lime flowers into a saucepan. Bring them to simmering point, cover the pan, and keep it on the lowest heat possible for 30 minutes. Remove from the heat and stir in the honey. Cover again and leave for 2 hours. Strain and bottle the cleanser. Store it in the refrigerator and use within 1 week.

Herbal Skin Toner

A toner splashed on to the face after cleansing will help to close the pores and invigorate the skin. The only ingredients you need are fresh or dried herbs and still, bottled spring water. Choose the herbs from the list on page 30.

1 ounce fresh herbs or 1 tbsp dried
1¼ cups still spring water

Put the herbs into a pitcher. Boil the water and pour it over the herbs. Cover with plastic wrap or a lid and leave to infuse for 2 hours. Line a strainer with cheesecloth or a coffee filter paper and strain the infusion through it. Store the toner in a covered jar in the refrigerator and use within a week.

Rosemary was one of the essential herbal ingredients of Hungary water. Use it for a herbal skin toner, a mouthwash, or in a rinse for your hair.

Mrs. C. F. Leyel, 1880–1957

Mrs. Leyel was the daughter of a teacher at Uppingham School, Rutland, in England, where her interest in flowers and herbs developed.
She intended to study medicine, but withdrew when faced with her first dissection, and instead joined a theater company and married a theatrical manager.
Attractive and vivacious, she was much involved in London society, but she maintained her passion for herbs and their uses.
When she became a widow in the 1920s, she began writing about herbs, and her many books include The Magic of Herbs, Herbal Delights, The Truth About Herbs, *and* The Gentle Art of Cookery. *She also built up a vast collection of old herbals. In 1929, on the death of Maud Grieve, Mrs. Leyel brought together and collated Mrs. Grieve's pamphlets on herbs to produce* A Modern Herbal *which was published in 1931. In 1927 Mrs. Leyel opened the first of her shops, Culpeper House, in Baker Street, London, selling herbal cosmetics, foods, and medicines. This was the start of the Culpeper chain, which continues today. Mrs. Leyel also founded the Society of Herbalists,*

and successfully fought for its existence when it was threatened by the Pharmacy and Medicines Bill of 1941, in England, which would have outlawed the practice of medical herbalism.

Inside Mrs. Leyel's first shop, Culpeper House, which opened in Baker Street, London, in 1927.

31

CULINARY HERBS

Herbs improve flavor and contain health-giving minerals, vitamins, and trace elements.

They provide a wide variety of taste for both savory and sweet dishes.

The first human beings were hunter-gatherers; they hunted wild animals and gathered plant foods. By trial and error they discovered how each plant tasted, whether it could be eaten in quantity, or whether it was better to scatter one or two leaves over fire-cooked meat. They also found out which herbs suited which meats, not only in terms of flavor but also by improving digestibility.

By the time earthenware cooking pots were in use around 10000 B.C., cereal and vegetable stews were the basic diet in many parts of the world. Salt was scarce and sharp-tasting green plants were used to provide extra flavor. They also supplied important vitamin C in seasons when wild fruit was not available. In Europe, the herbs most often used at this time were nettles, plantain, mallows, docks, ramsons (wild garlic), wild leeks, and chives. Thick stews, cooked in a pot over an open fire, remained the main food of the ordinary people for many centuries, becoming known much later as *pottages*.

In medieval times the most common dish in ordinary households was *pottage* flavored with green herbs, including orache (Atriplex, or goosefoot), clary (a type of mint), mallow, dock, and bugloss (borage), plus the sage, parsley, thyme, mints, and fennel we would recognize today. A *pottage* that was colored green with the many herbs used was called *joutes*. It was also sometimes eaten as a sauce.

By the 17th century, the large-leaved wild herbs, such as mallow and bugloss, gave way to new vegetables, such as spinach, and only country people collected nettles and turnip tops. French recipe books began to recommend mixtures of what they called "sweet" or "fine" herbs, which meant the herbs of mainly Mediterranean origin that we would regard as culinary herbs today. They included thyme, marjoram, oregano, basil, rosemary, savory, parsley, and sage. The French recommendations influenced cooks all over Europe and, particularly after the Restoration, English cookbooks began to give the instruction "take a faggot of sweet herbs."

Sage has long been known as a herb for rich meats, both to add flavor and to make them more digestible.

32

In medieval times a great quantity of meat was eaten in rich households. Large amounts of herbs and spices were used to disguise its flavor when it was not very fresh.

Joutes

Take borage, violet, mallows, parsley, young worts, beet, avens, bugloss, with orache and others, pick them clean, and cast them on a vessel, and boyl them a good while; then take them and presse them on a fair board, and hew them right small, and put white bread thereto, and grind withal; and then cast them into a fair pot, and [pour in] good fresh broth enough thereto through a strainer.

15TH-CENTURY MANUSCRIPT

Spices such as nutmeg became more readily available in Europe by the mid-18th century. For a time the use of mace and nutmeg almost replaced herbs completely.

By the mid-18th century, thick *pottages*, made with a mixture of both small and large leaved plants, had virtually disappeared and cooks relied on the "sweet herbs" for most of their dishes. Spices became more readily available, and spices such as mace and nutmeg often replaced herbs completely. In the 18th century there was a vogue for making bottled sauces, which were kept in the kitchen ready for use as instant flavorings and in gravies.

In the 19th century, the same "sweet herbs" were being referred to by some cooks as "savory herbs." In England, they were put into stuffings, sauces, and soups and occasionally into salads, but interest in them was waning. Mrs. Beeton, writing in 1891, appears not to have been enthusiastic about herbs, and in the United States Fanny Farmer's cook book uses them even less. Bottled sauces and a flavoring called Poultry Seasoning seem to have been the order of the day. In France and other European countries, such as Spain and Italy, herbs were used far more generously and they have always been popular.

That remained the case until the 1960s. By then there were so many commercial foods containing artificial flavorings on the market that people began to realize they were missing the natural taste and the health-giving qualities of fresh herbs. This lack of taste became more obvious as people increasingly traveled around the world and sampled the cuisine of other countries. The foods, flavorings, and seasonings of ethnic groups have spilled over from specialist stores and markets to become common ingredients available to everyone. Herbs have once again become essential components of our diet.

A powdering mill used in New York kitchens in the 1850s for reducing herbs and roots into powdered form.

33

Green Dumplings: Mrs. Lord's Receipt

Slice a pound of the crume [crumb] of browne bread, then haveing your pott boyleing with beef scume off ye fatt and put to it ye bread in which let it soake an houre, then beate it with a spoone very small, then put in 5 eggs whites and all and a little ginger and sweet herbs shred small, whereof tow parts must be penneroyall stir it all together and strew in flower with three quarters of a pound of suet cutt very small; then haveing a little flower rubed one ye palmes of ye hands role them rounde and put them into ye pott when it boyls very fast three quarters of an howre boyles them.

Herbs in the Kitchen

To flavor or garnish food, herbs can be used whole,

as sprigs or leaves, or chopped.

When preparing fresh herbs, cut sprigs from the plant carefully with sharp scissors; rinse the sprigs in cold water, and shake them dry. If you are using whole leaves—as a garnish, for example—choose the most attractive ones from the plant.

When chopping herbs, whether you can use or discard the stems depends on the herb. For shrubby herbs with woody stems, such as thyme, winter savory, or rosemary, it is best to remove the stems completely. Small, hard pieces of stem are unpleasant in any dish. Where the stems are soft, as in parsley or chervil, you can chop the tops of the stems with the leaves. In all cases, you should have more leaf than stem.

To chop herbs you need a sharp, heavy chopping knife, or a mezzaluna, and a chopping board. For a large-leaved herb, begin by holding the leaves together with one hand and slicing with the other. Once the pieces are

A basket of thyme and freshly cut fennel, rosemary, mint, and parsley, ready for cooking aromatic dishes.

34

small enough, hold the knife blade with both hands and chop quickly and sharply over the herb until it is finely chopped.

BOUQUET GARNI

A bouquet garni is made from a selection of herbs tied together. It is used to flavor dishes such as soups and stews as they cook. Choose the herbs to suit the other ingredients of the dish; for example, a sprig each of parsley, thyme, and marjoram for a chicken casserole. Add a bay leaf or a small strip of leek. Tie the bouquet together with string, leaving a loop long enough to hold it by. Put the bouquet garni into a dish, such as a casserole, soup, or braised dish, and remove it before serving.

USES OF HERBS

Herbs will add extra flavor and interest to a wide variety of dishes from soups to desserts. See below for suggestions of how to use herbs with each dish.

SOUPS: Add a bouquet garni to the soup at the beginning of cooking time, and remove it before blending if the soup is to be a smooth one or before serving if not. Garnish the soup with chopped herbs.

CASSEROLES, STEWS, AND BRAISED DISHES: Flavor with chopped herbs or a bouquet garni while

To make a coole tankett [tankard]—take a quart of Renish wine, or whitewine and put to it a pinte of fayre water; and 2 Lemmons, sweeten it to your likeing with good suger; and put on it some Burage [borage], Baume [lemon balm], and Burnett, if you please. Let ye Lemmon pill be cutt hansomely some to be in ye wine and some to hang on ye tankett.

REBECCA PRICE, 17TH CENTURY

Costmary Conserve

Pick the flowers when they are dry, only use the petals, weigh them and to every pound of petals take two pounds and a half of loaf sugar. Beat the two together in a stone mortar, adding the sugar by degrees. When well incorporated, press into gallipots without first boiling. Tie over paper and leather on top of the paper and it will keep seven years.

HANNAH GLASSE, 1747

Parsley

*The excellency of this herb
accordeth with the frequent use
thereof. For there is almost no
meat or sauce which will not have
Perseley either in it or about it.*

FROM DYET'S *DRY DINNER*, 1599

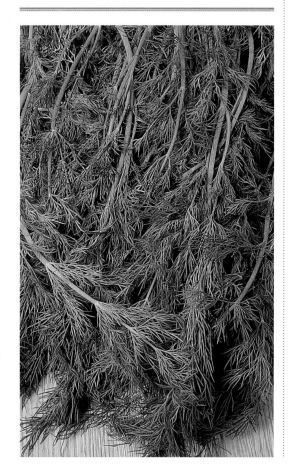

*The delicate
appearance of chives
gives a clue to their
gentle, onionlike flavor.
Fresh chives can be
picked from March
to October.*

*The beautiful,
feathery leaves of dill have
a strong, pungent aroma.
They often give flavor to
cucumber pickles and
to Gravad Lax, the
Scandinavian dish of
raw, marinated salmon.*

cooking. Garnish with chopped herbs before serving.

ROASTS: Lay sprigs of herbs over roasting meats, or make a crispy, herb-flavored coating.

PATES: Add chopped herbs to the mixture before cooking.

STUFFINGS: Mix chopped herbs with bread crumbs when making stuffings.

PASTA: Add herb sprigs to the cooking water and remove before serving. Toss cooked pasta in oil or butter flavored with garlic and chopped herbs. Use herbs in pasta sauces.

RICE: Fork chopped herbs into cooked rice.

VEGETABLE DISHES: Sprinkle chopped herbs over roasting vegetables. Add herb sprigs or a bouquet garni to the water for boiling vegetables. Put chopped herbs in vegetable casseroles. Garnish cooked vegetables with chopped herbs.

SALADS: Add chopped herbs to salad dressings. Garnish salads with whole leaves or sprigs.

SWEET DISHES: Add sprigs to stewing fruit as it cooks. Flavor sugar syrups and milk for desserts with fresh sprigs. Garnish sweet dishes with whole leaves and sprigs.

HERB GARNISHES

The appearance of many dishes can instantly be enhanced with the addition of chopped herbs, herb sprigs, or herb leaves. The garnish can be wholly or partly eaten with the dish and thereby improves the overall flavor.

Chopped fresh herbs make an attractive contrast in color when sprinkled over a variety of cooked dishes, including casseroles, stews, and braised dishes; broiled or sautéed dishes; soups; pasta and rice; and vegetable dishes.

Whole leaves, such as those of parsley, chervil, coriander or cilantro, basil, and mint, can be arranged singly or in patterns, either on the food or on the plate, when serving pâtés, fish steaks and fillets, meat chops, first courses cooked in individual dishes, and sorbets and ice creams.

Larger herb leaves can also be used as a base for individual portions. Place a scoop of ice cream on a bed of balm leaves, for example, or use a bed of arugula leaves for a small dish of shrimp.

The most attractive herb sprigs are fennel, dill, tarragon, parsley, and chervil. These are mostly used for garnishes only and are best for dishes that are taken to the table before being served on individual plates, such as whole poached fish or a joint of roast chicken.

CHOOSING THE RIGHT HERBS

There is a herb for every ingredient. These are some of the most popular combinations:

BEEF: parsley, thyme, bay, winter savory.

LAMB: thyme, lemon thyme, mint, marjoram, oregano, rosemary, tarragon, sorrel, bay.

PORK: sage, rosemary, fennel, lovage.

CHICKEN/TURKEY: parsley, thyme, lemon thyme, balm, marjoram, tarragon, fennel, bay, coriander or cilantro, chives, sorrel.

DUCK: sage, mint, marjoram, thyme, parsley.

GOOSE: sage, parsley, marjoram, thyme.

GAME: parsley, marjoram, thyme, winter savory, tarragon.

WHITE FISH: parsley, fennel, dill, tarragon, coriander or cilantro, chives, basil, lemon thyme, balm, lemon verbena.

OILY FISH: dill, fennel, chives, mint, balm, sorrel, thyme, lemon thyme.

CHEESE DISHES: parsley, thyme, sage, mint, sorrel.

EGGS: parsley, chervil, tarragon, chives, fennel.

LEGUMES: parsley, marjoram, thyme, fennel, coriander or cilantro, chives, basil, bay.

Herbs are so full of sunshine and sweetness that it seems there can be no tonic like them, and it is curious how appreciative invalids are of sweet scented herbs. Flower scents are often too heavy for them, but a bunch of fragrant herbs seems a perpetual joy.

ELEANOR SINCLAIR RHODE, *A GARDEN OF HERBS*, 1920s

To Stuff a Chine of Pork

Make a stuffing of the fat Leaf of Pork, Parsley, Thyme, Sage, Eggs and Crumbs of Bread, season it with Pepper, Salt, Shalot, and Nutmeg, and stuff it thick; then roast it gently.

HANNAH GLASSE, 1747

VEGETABLE DISHES: parsley, chervil, marjoram, oregano, thyme, lemon thyme, balm, basil, lovage, dill.

SALADS: parsley, chervil, chives, coriander or cilantro, basil, arugula, fennel, dill, balm, dandelion leaves.

PASTA: basil, parsley, oregano, thyme, rosemary, marjoram.

RICE: parsley, coriander or cilantro, mint.

SWEET DISHES: mint, peppermint, sweet cicely, angelica, balm, lemon thyme, scented geranium, lavender.

FRESH OR DRIED

There is nothing to beat the flavor of fresh herbs but, especially if you grow your own, there will be certain times of the year when they are not available. There are certain recipes, such as those for salads, in which dried herbs are not suitable. However, dried herbs can be substituted for fresh in dishes that require slow cooking, such as soups or casseroles. Generally speaking, because the flavor of dried herbs is very concentrated, about one-third the amount of dried herbs is equivalent to the amount of fresh herbs stipulated in a recipe.

CHAPTER ONE

APPETIZERS
AND SNACKS

ttractive as garnishes and
exciting as flavorings, herbs are
the perfect ingredient for small,
interesting dishes to start a meal. Fresh
or dried, in hot or in cold dishes, they
wake up taste buds and stimulate
the appetite.

APPETIZERS AND SNACKS

Soups, vegetables, pasta, pâtés, and light egg and meat dishes all make ideal first courses; a variety of fresh herbs lend a special touch to their flavor and appearance. Add chopped herbs to a soup just before reheating or serving, so the two flavors blend but the herbs stay fresh. Try parsley with mushroom soup, the crisp tang of dill with creamy pumpkin, or spicy lovage with potato.

Vegetables prepared in a special way always make good appetizers. Fill eggplants with a rich mixture of tomatoes flavored with fresh oregano. Use arugula as an outstanding contrast to a rich, creamy sauce for pasta, or add tarragon to sour cream to make an unusual dip for crispy coated small pieces of chicken breast.

Pâtés are always popular. Flavor shrimp pâté with coriander or cilantro, or make an unusual light pâté of farmer cheese and flageolet beans seasoned with mint. Instead of serving plain toast as an accompaniment, try crispy, golden, herbed bread sticks.

Eggs make delicious appetizers and snacks. Use them for a mushroom and herb quiche, or for tiny omelets to serve with marinated olives. For a really substantial snack, prepare herbed crêpes filled with goat cheese.

A wealthy family's kitchen in the middle ages, as illustrated in an Italian Breviary (a book of psalms, hymns, and prayers), 15th-century manuscript.

SUMMER SAVORY *and* CARAMELIZED ONION FRITTATA *with* MARINATED OLIVES

A frittata is a flat, unfolded omelet. It can be eaten hot or cold and is ideal for summer lunches and picnics. To take it on a picnic, simply wrap the whole frittata in foil and slice it on arrival. Summer savory is a herb that has been used since the days of the Romans.

SERVES 4

1tbsp butter
1tbsp olive oil
2 large red onions, thinly sliced
6 eggs, beaten
2 to 3tbsp roughly chopped summer savory
Salt and freshly ground black pepper

MARINATED OLIVES
1½ cups mixed, unpitted black and green olives
1tbsp finely chopped fresh oregano
3tbsp olive oil
2tsp crushed coriander seeds
1tbsp lemon juice
1 small red chili, thinly sliced and seeded

First marinate the olives. Place all the ingredients in a jar with a tightly fitting lid and shake well. Leave to marinate for several hours or, if possible, overnight in the refrigerator. Remove from the refrigerator at least 30 minutes before serving to allow the olives to reach room temperature.

Heat the butter and oil in a skillet and add the onions. Cook over very low heat for 30 to 40 minutes, until the onions have turned golden and caramelized. Spread them out over the bottom of the pan and increase the heat to medium. Season the eggs and stir in the summer savory. Pour the eggs into the pan, over the onions. Stir a couple of times, to incorporate the onions, and then cook over medium heat for about 5 minutes, until the edges begin to set. Preheat the broiler to medium-high.

Once the bottom of the frittata has begun to set, put the pan under the hot broiler. Broil until the frittata is set and lightly browned on top.

To serve, slice into wedges or cubes, and serve accompanied by a green salad with fresh herb salad dressing (page 121) and the marinated olives.

GOUJONS OF CHICKEN *with a* SOUR CREAM *and* HERB DIP

Serve these flavorful chicken pieces as an appetizer, a light snack, or as part of a buffet. The sour-cream dipping sauce uses tarragon, which goes particularly well with chicken.

SERVES 4

Oil for deep-frying
4 large skinless, boneless chicken breast halves
3tbsp minced fresh mixed herbs
2½ cups fresh white bread crumbs, seasoned
⅓ cup all-purpose flour, seasoned
3 eggs, beaten

DIPPING SAUCE
⅔ cup sour cream
2tbsp minced fresh tarragon
1 small garlic clove, crushed
1tbsp lemon juice
1tbsp wholegrain mustard
Pinch of salt and ground white pepper

First make the dipping sauce. Combine all the ingredients in a small bowl and set aside while you make the chicken, to let the flavors develop.

Heat the oil in a deep-fryer or large saucepan to 375°F, or until a cube of day-old bread browns in 30 seconds.

Cut the chicken into thin strips, about 4 × ¾ inches. Combine the mixed herbs with the bread crumbs. Put the flour and bread crumbs on two separate plates and put the beaten eggs in a shallow dish. Dip the pieces of chicken first into the flour, then into the egg, and finally into the bread crumbs.

Once the oil is hot enough, fry the chicken a few pieces at a time for 3 to 4 minutes, until crisp and golden. Drain on paper towels and keep warm in a low oven while you cook the rest of the chicken.

Serve accompanied by the sour cream and herb dipping sauce.

43

POTATO *and* LOVAGE SOUP

Lovage is particularly suited to cooking with root vegetables, potatoes in particular. It has a celerylike flavor, and if you are unable to find it, celery is a good substitute.

SERVES 4

2tbsp olive oil	*Salt and freshly ground black*
1 onion, chopped	* pepper*
3 cups peeled and cubed	*Crusty bread or croutons, to*
* potatoes*	* serve*
⅔ to 1¼ cups milk	
2 to 3tbsp minced fresh lovage,	*TO GARNISH*
* or 2 sticks minced celery*	*Lovage or celery leaves*

Heat the oil in a large saucepan and add the onion and potatoes. If using celery instead of lovage, add the chopped celery to the onion and potatoes. Cook over low heat for 10 minutes. Pour in 3 cups water and simmer, until the potatoes are tender. Remove from the heat and leave to cool slightly.

Purée in a food processor. Return to a clean pan, season, and stir in the lovage and enough milk to make the desirable consistency. Heat through, scatter lovage or celery leaves over the soup, and serve immediately, accompanied by crusty bread or croutons.

SHRIMP *and* CILANTRO PÂTÉ

If you're looking for an elegant appetizer you can prepare in advance, this recipe is the answer. Prepare it in the morning and leave it to chill until just before you serve it. Cilantro has a very distinctive flavor but it doesn't overwhelm the more subtle flavor of the shrimp in this dish.

SERVES 4

6tbsp butter	*1tbsp lemon juice (optional)*
1 garlic clove, crushed	*Salt and freshly ground black*
3 green onions, sliced	* pepper*
1½ lb raw shrimp in their	
* shells, defrosted if frozen,*	
* peeled*	*TO GARNISH*
4tbsp roughly chopped fresh	*1tbsp roughly chopped fresh*
* cilantro leaves*	* cilantro leaves*
3tbsp heavy cream	

Melt the butter in a saucepan and very gently sauté the garlic and onions for 2 minutes, without browning the garlic. Remove the pan from the heat, add the shrimp, and stir to coat the shrimp in the butter mixture. Transfer to a food processor and add the cilantro leaves. Use the pulse button to process for about 10 seconds, so the mixture remains coarsely textured. Add the cream, lemon juice (if using), and seasoning and pulse a couple more times. Spoon the pâté into individual serving dishes and chill for several hours. Alternatively, line 4 ramekins with plastic wrap and fill them with pâté. Chill until you want to serve and then turn out onto serving plates.

To serve, sprinkle the chopped cilantro over each portion of pâté and offer Melba toast.

Pedanius Dioscorides, 1st century

Born in Greece in the 1st century A.D., Dioscorides became a Roman army surgeon, traveling with Nero's armies. Realizing that there was no book recording all the contemporary information on plants and other drugs, he set about compiling one, and produced in Greek Peri Hulas Iatrikes, *or "About Medicinal Trees". It was translated into Latin as* De Materia Medica *or "About Medical Materials."*
The work illustrated and described the many medicinal plants that Dioscorides and his colleagues had discovered on their travels. It outlined their medicinal qualities and gave advice and warnings about their

application. Although there was some information about animal and mineral-based drugs, it was the section on plants that made Dioscorides famous.

MUSHROOM SOUP *with* PARSLEY

This is a soup that is versatile enough to be served at an elegant dinner party, but which would not be out of place at a simple family supper. Add the garnish of wild mushrooms for a dinner party and sprinkle with chopped fresh parsley.

SERVES 4

½oz dried porcini
  (ceps)
4tbsp butter
4 shallots, chopped
1 garlic clove, crushed
10oz large, flat-cap
  mushrooms, thickly sliced
⅔ cup dry white wine
2 cups chicken or vegetable
  stock
3tbsp minced fresh parsley
3 to 5tbsp light cream

Salt and freshly ground black
  pepper

TO GARNISH
¾ cup wiped and torn mixed
  wild mushrooms, such as
  chanterelles, and ceps
  (optional)
1tbsp chopped fresh parsley

TO SERVE
Crusty bread

Soak the dried porcini in 1¼ cups hot water for 20 minutes, then strain, reserving the liquid. Strain the liquid once more through a cheesecloth-lined strainer and chop the soaked mushrooms.

Over medium heat, melt 3 tablespoons of the butter in a large saucepan and gently sauté the shallots for 5 minutes. Stir in the garlic and sauté for 2 minutes longer. Add the sliced mushrooms and cook gently, covered, for about 5 minutes. Pour in the wine and bring to a boil; boil rapidly for 2 minutes to reduce the wine. Pour in the stock and mushroom-soaking liquid. Add the soaked mushrooms and seasoning and simmer for about 15 minutes.

Remove from the heat and leave to cool slightly. Purée in a food processor until smooth.

Return to a clean pan, stir in the parsley and cream and check the seasoning. Gently reheat.

Meanwhile, if you are making the wild-mushroom garnish, melt the remaining butter in a pan and add the wild mushrooms. Cook gently for about 5 minutes, until softened.

To serve, pour the mushroom soup into warmed, individual soup bowls and garnish with a few wild mushrooms and a sprinkling of parsley. Serve immediately with crusty bread.

GRAPE *and* CUCUMBER COOLER

Borage has the refreshing taste of cucumber and conjures up memories of old-fashioned summer garden parties. It is frequently used to garnish summer drinks, in particular the quintessentially British Pimms.

MAKES ABOUT 1 QUART

1½ lemons
3 to 4tbsp sugar
1¼ cups orange
  juice, chilled
1¼ cups red grape
  juice, chilled
2 cups sparkling
  water, chilled
Ice cubes

TO GARNISH
Cucumber slices
½ lemon
Fresh borage sprigs

Squeeze the juice from 1½ lemons and slice the remaining half-lemon into thin slices. In a pitcher or large bowl, combine the sugar with the orange, lemon, and grape juices and stir until the sugar dissolves. Add the water and mix well. Add the ice cubes and garnish with slices of cucumber and lemon, and sprigs of borage.

MINT JULEP

This is a traditional drink from the southern states. It is refreshing served on a hot day and is meant to be sipped slowly.

SERVES 1

10 sprigs of mint,
  leaves only
1tsp sugar

2tbsp water
4tbsp brandy,
  whiskey, or
  bourbon
Crushed ice

Crush half the mint, with the sugar and water, in a small pitcher and mix to extract the mint flavor. Fill a glass with the crushed ice and strain the mint mixture over, discarding the mint leaves. Pour in the chosen liquor and stir gently to mix the drink. Garnish with remaining sprigs of mint.

NONALCOHOLIC SUMMER PUNCH

On a balmy summer's day, often there is nothing better than a refreshing drink with a hint of fresh herbs. This punch is ideal as it is nonalcoholic, so it leaves your head clear to concentrate on other more pressing matters, such as gardening or sunbathing!

46

MAKES ABOUT 2½ QUARTS

2 ½ cups orange juice, chilled
2 ½ cups tropical fruit juice, chilled
5 cups lemonade, chilled
Ice cubes

1 peach, halved and sliced
12 strawberries, hulled and quartered
Fresh balm and mint sprigs, to garnish

Mix the orange juice and tropical fruit juices with the lemonade in a jug or punch bowl. Add the ice cubes and fruit, and garnish with the sprigs of balm and mint. Serve at once.

HERB TEA

Many fresh or dried herbs can be made into refreshing teas, including chamo-mile, mint, thyme, rosemary, savory, and borage.

SERVES 1

2tbsp chopped fresh herb, such as mint, or 1tbsp dried herb
1 cup boiling water

To Serve
Lemon slices
Sugar

Steep your chosen herb in the boiling water for 4–5 minutes. Strain and serve with slices of lemon and sugar, to taste.

ALCOHOLIC SUMMER PUNCH

If you are catering for large numbers, it is often much easier to prepare a big bowl of punch, rather than serve a wide range of individual drinks. If you need a very large quantity, make it all up beforehand and store in containers until you are ready to decant it into a punch bowl or glass pitcher.

MAKES ABOUT 2½ QUARTS

3¾ cups tropical fruit juice, chilled
8tbsp brandy
2 bottles sparkling dry white wine, chilled

1 lime, sliced
1 orange, sliced
Fresh mint sprigs
Fresh borage sprigs
Ice cubes

Mix together the fruit juice, brandy, and white wine and add 1 or 2 slices of the lime and orange and a sprig or two of mint and borage. Chill in the refrigerator for at least 1 hour.

Just before serving, remove the herbs and add the remaining slices of fruit and sprigs of mint and borage. Add a few ice cubes to keep the punch cool and serve.

PUMPKIN *and* DILL SOUP

Pumpkin is a delightful vegetable that is under-used in cooking, but is, of course, a common sight around Halloween. Dill is particularly suited to soups made with root and winter vegetables; add it toward the end of cooking to retain maximum flavour.

SERVES 4

2tbsp butter
2tbsp olive or vegetable oil
1 onion, roughly chopped
1½lb pumpkin, peeled, seeded, and chopped
1 cup milk
1 to 2tbsp roughly chopped fresh dill

Salt and freshly ground black pepper

CROUTONS
3 slices of white bread, crusts removed, and cut into ½-inch cubes

Preheat the oven to 425°F. Melt the butter and oil in a large saucepan and add the onion and pumpkin. Cook over a low heat for about 10 minutes. Pour in 2 cups hot water. Simmer gently, for 15 to 20 minutes, until the pumpkin is very tender.

Meanwhile, to make the croutons, put the cubes of bread in a bowl and pour over the oil. Season with salt and pepper and toss well. Spread the bread out on a baking sheet and bake for 5 to 10 minutes, until crisp.

When the pumpkin is tender, allow it to cool slightly. Push it through a strainer, or purée in a food processor. Return to a clean saucepan and stir in the milk. Bring to a boil, then stir in the dill and seasoning.

Serve with the croutons or with crusty bread.

Equipment for Chopping Herbs

No special equipment is needed for chopping herbs. A large, heavy kitchen knife with a sharp, triangular-shaped blade, like the kind used for chopping vegetables, is perfectly adequate when combined with a sturdy chopping board.

However, especially made herb-chopping knives are available. One of the most popular is a curved knife with a handle at each end, sometimes called a herb-chopper or mezzaluna. These come single-bladed (usually 8 inches long) or double-bladed (about 6 inches long) with two parallel blades attached together to the handles. To use a mezzaluna on a chopping board, rock it from side to side over the herbs. Some are supplied with a bowl, into which they fit neatly. Put the herbs into the bowl and press the mezzaluna down on them repeatedly to chop them.

Also available is a herb mill, consisting of a small cylindrical container, which is filled with herbs, and a grinder. The herbs are minced by turning a handle.

48

PASTA *with* ARUGULA *and* DOLCELATTE

Arugula is making a spectacular revival in American and British cooking, which is most welcome because this dandelion-shaped herb is delicious served in salads, tossed into pasta, and even thrown fresh onto pizzas!

SERVES 4

10oz dry rigatoni
2tbsp olive oil
1 small onion, minced
1 fat garlic clove, quartered
⅔ cup dry white wine
1 cup cubed dolcelatte cheese

1 cup heavy cream
3oz arugula leaves, long stems removed
Salt and freshly ground black pepper

Cook the pasta in a large pot of boiling water for 10 to 12 minutes, until tender. Drain and keep warm.

Over medium heat, heat the oil in a large saucepan. Add the onion and fry gently for 8 minutes, until the onion is soft. Stir in the garlic and fry for 2 minutes longer. Add the wine, increase the heat, and simmer for about 4 minutes, until the wine has reduced to a syrupy consistency. Reduce the heat to medium, then stir in the cubes of dolcelatte and the cream. Stir gently to let the dolcelatte to melt slightly. Season with salt and freshly ground black pepper. Add the cooked pasta and mix well, coating the pasta with the sauce. Stir in half the arugula and transfer to a warmed serving dish. Scatter the remaining arugula over and serve immediately.

Herb *and* Mushroom Quiche

Often passed over for more fashionable foods, a well-flavored quiche can be absolutely delicious. Here, a variety of herbs have been suggested but, if some aren't available, use what can be found. This is an ideal dish for taking on picnics or for serving at summer parties. Serve hot or at room temperature, accompanied by salad.

SERVES 4–6

12oz basic piecrust dough	*4tbsp minced fresh herbs, such*
2tbsp butter	*as basil, parsley, chives, and*
2 cups roughly chopped flat-cap	*oregano*
mushrooms	*1tbsp minced fresh thyme leaves*
3 eggs	*Salt and freshly ground black*
⅔ cup milk	*pepper*

This quiche can be made in an 8 × 1¼-inch round pan or a 9 × 1-inch round pan with a loose bottom. Roll out the dough to a circle 3 inches wider than the pan. Line the pan and trim the edges. Prick the bottom all over with a fork and chill in the refrigerator for at least 30 minutes while you prepare the filling.

Preheat the oven to 375°F. To make the filling, melt the butter in a saucepan and add the chopped mushrooms. Cook, uncovered, for about 5 minutes, until the mushrooms have released their juices and the juices have all but evaporated. Set aside.

Beat the eggs with the milk and stir in the chopped herbs (reserving the thyme) and seasoning.

Put the pan on a baking sheet, to make it easier to transfer the quiche in and out of the oven. Line the pan with waxed paper and fill it with baking beans or dried beans. Bake for 10 minutes. Remove the beans and paper and pour half the filling into the pastry shell, then scatter the mushrooms over. Pour the remaining filling over, sprinkle with the chopped thyme, and bake for 35 to 40 minutes, until the filling is set and the top is golden brown. Leave to cool for at least 5 minutes on a wire rack.

Nicholas Culpeper, 1616–54

Nicholas Culpeper provided us with one of the most-read herbals of all time—the result of a tragic love affair which caused his life to change direction.
The son of an English rector, Nicholas Culpeper studied for several years at Cambridge University until he fell in love. The couple decided to elope, so he borrowed £200 from his mother (a substantial sum in those days) and arranged to meet his partner near Lewes, in Sussex, in southern England, where they intended to marry. On the way, she was struck by lightning and killed.
Culpeper was too traumatized to settle to the grandeur of Cambridge society or the formalities of his education, so his grandfather paid a London apothecary £50 to employ Nicholas as an apprentice.
After some years Nicholas set up his own practice in the Spitalfields area of London, then a run-down district which was home to the poorest of the poor. Unlike conventional doctors, who would not dispense their expensive chemical potions without payment, Culpeper made himself the poor people's doctor, treating them from his own clinic with local herbs and very often waiving the fee.
His dislike of established medical practice gained him many enemies in the profession, but this did not prevent him from publishing a herbal which he entitled The English Physician. *In it he described numerous readily available and easily grown herbs, together with the remedies they could provide. It became indispensable for housewives, who were responsible for their families' health, and is still one of the most popular herbals.*

51

Sweet Marjoram Crêpes

Filled crêpes make a substantial appetizer or snack. Serve on their own or with a few dressed salad leaves.

SERVES 4

1 cup unsifted all-purpose flour	FILLING
Pinch of salt	*7oz soft goat cheese, rind removed, if necessary*
1 egg	*3 to 4tbsp milk*
1¼ cups milk	*2 firm ripe tomatoes, blanched, peeled, seeded, and chopped*
1tbsp butter, melted	*8 to 10 fresh basil leaves, torn*
3tbsp minced fresh sweet marjoram	*Salt and freshly ground black pepper*
Butter for frying	*½ cup pitted black olives, roughly chopped*

To make the crêpes, put the flour and salt in a bowl and make a well in the middle. Add the egg and, using an electric mixer on low speed, start to incorporate the flour into the egg. Gradually pour in the milk and continue beating until a smooth batter forms. Stir in the melted butter and strain the batter through a strainer into a pitcher. Stir in the chopped marjoram. Cover and chill for 1 hour.

Preheat the oven to 375°F. Meanwhile, make the filling. Soften the cheese to a spreadable consistency by adding a little of the milk and beating well. Add as much milk as is necessary and then mix the cheese with the remaining filling ingredients.

Put a 7-inch crêpe pan or skillet over high heat. When the pan is very hot, melt a small knob of butter in it and swirl it around. Reduce the heat to medium and pour or ladle in about 2 tablespoons of batter, swirling it around to cover the bottom of the pan. Cook for 1 to 1½ minutes, or less if the crêpes cook quicker. When the edges are brown, use a spatula to loosen the crêpe. Flip it over and cook the other side for 1 minute longer. Transfer the crêpe to a warmed plate and continue until all the batter is used up or you have 8 crêpes.

Divide the filling mixture between 8 crêpes (freeze any remaining ones) and carefully spread it out to cover the crêpe, leaving a 1-inch border around the edge. Roll up the crêpes and put them in a single layer in a greased baking dish. Warm in the preheated oven for 10 minutes. Serve immediately.

Baked Eggplant *with* Basil *and* Oregano

Eggplants are eaten in many nations and are found in abundance in Mediterranean, Asian, and Middle Eastern cooking. This is a rich, exotic dish, good for hot, summery days in the garden and for cold winter-evening dinner parties, as it can be served hot or chilled.

SERVES 4

2 eggplants	*5oz mozzarella cheese, thinly sliced*
4tbsp olive oil	*3tbsp freshly grated Parmesan cheese*
2 garlic cloves, crushed	
1 onion, minced	*Salt and freshly ground black pepper*
13oz-can crushed tomatoes	
2tsp sugar	*Small basil leaves, to garnish*
6 fresh basil leaves, roughly torn	
1tbsp minced fresh oregano, or 2tsp dried oregano	

Preheat the oven to 375°F. Cut each eggplant in half lengthwise and scoop out the flesh from each one, leaving at least an ½-inch edge of flesh around the edge, to prevent the eggplant from falling apart during cooking. Roughly chop half the scooped-out flesh and discard the other half.

Heat 1 tablespoon of the oil in a small saucepan and gently sauté the garlic and onion for 3 to 4 minutes, until the onions are soft. Add the tomatoes and eggplant flesh and bring to a boil. Stir in the sugar and seasoning and boil hard for about 5 minutes, to reduce the sauce; stir frequently to prevent the sauce burning. Remove from the heat and stir in the basil and oregano.

Spoon some of the mikxture into each eggplant shell; top with slices of mozzarella cheese and sprinkle with Parmesan cheese. Drizzle the remaining oil over. Put on a baking sheet and bake for 50 to 60 minutes, until the cheese has formed a delicious golden crust on the top of each eggplant half.

Serve the eggplant hot, at room temperature, or chilled, garnished with small basil leaves.

MINTED BEAN *and* HERB PÂTÉ *with* HERBED "BREAD STICKS"

This is a light, fresh-tasting pâté that can be made very quickly in the food processor. The toasted bread is an unusual alternative to Melba toast or crusty bread.

SERVES 4

13oz-can of flageolet beans, drained and rinsed
1 cup farmer cheese
3tbsp plain yogurt
4tbsp roughly chopped fresh mint
1tsp chili powder
8 slices white bread, crusts removed

3tbsp olive oil
3tbsp minced mixed fresh herbs, such as oregano, parsley, thyme, and marjoram
Salt and freshly ground black pepper
4 sprigs fresh mint, to garnish

Preheat the oven to 375°F. Put the beans, farmer cheese, yogurt, mint, and seasoning into a food processor and purée until fairly smooth but still with a bit of texture. Transfer to ramekins or individual serving bowls.

To make the "bread sticks," cut each slice of bread into strips approximately ¾ inch wide. Combine the olive oil with the herbs. Toss the bread sticks in the oil and herbs, until evenly coated. Transfer to a baking sheet or baking dish. Bake for 10 minutes, until golden. Garnish each pâté with a sprig of mint and serve with the bread.

53

Lavender

*Lavender is one of the most versatile of herbs. It has been loved for centuries for
its fresh, sweet scent, its healing abilities, and even its culinary properties.*

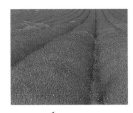

*A field of English
lavender just before
harvesting. After the
fragrant flower spikes
have been cut, some are
dried for lavender bags
and potpourri and the
rest go through a
distilling process to
make lavender oil.*

There are two main types of lavender:
Lavandula angustifolia (also called *L. vera*,
L. officinalis, or *L. spica*), which is the one
most grown commercially; and *Lavandula
latifolia* (also known as spike or wild lavender).

Lavender comes from the hilly regions of the
western Mediterranean and it was taken all
over Europe by the Romans, for whom it was
one of the most favored plants. It is now grown
commercially in France, particularly in
Provence, Italy, England, Norway, Australia,
and the United States.

Lavender is cut when the flowers are fully
open and the oil content is greatest. It was once
harvested by teams of women with sickles but
now it is mainly gathered mechanically. Spaces
of about 7 feet are left between the rows to
allow the machines to pass, and the harvester
travels between the
lines of lavender, lift-
ing the stems and
cutting and bagging
the flowerheads.

Some of the lavender
is dried by being laid
on a ventilated floor in
a drying shed and
having warm air pum-
ped around it until the
flowers are crisp.
The rest is put
through a process of
steam distillation to
draw off the richly
scented, golden col-
ored oil.

You can use dried
lavender flowers with
their fresh scent for
potpourris and for making cosmetics, lavender
bags, and bath preparations.

Dried or fresh lavender is also used in the
kitchen. Many dried mixtures labeled "herbes
de Provence," intended for use in omelets and
casseroles, contain a little lavender, and it adds

*Englishwomen have forgotten, if
they ever knew, that it is the scent
par excellence of England, and
that its aroma is more pleasing to
Englishmen than any other, and
more health-giving.*

Mrs. C. F. Leyel, *The Magic of Herbs*, 1926

Lavender Bottles

*These are also called lavender wands.
Hang them up in a closet or place them
in a drawer with your clothes. To make
one bottle, cut 20 lavender sprigs with
the flowers open and with long
stems. Trim the stems to the same
length and strip off any side
shoots or leaves. Tie the
bunch of lavender at the
bottom of the heads and
fold the stems down over
the heads, spacing them
evenly. Tie the stems
again at the bottom of the
flower heads. Make another tie at the
bottom of the stems. Cover the cotton
ties with ribbon, making a loop at the
stem end for hanging. Alternatively,
weave ribbon in and out of the stems to
enclose the flowers and cover the stems.*

*A lavender field in Provence with the plants grown
in rows to make mechanical harvesting easy.*

54

Plantations of lavender make the air smell very sweet in the summer months. Here they surround a farm in Vaucluse, France.

a special touch to deserts, such as ice creams and fruit salads.

The healing properties of lavender and lavender oil are many. The scent is both refreshing and relaxing, and it can ease headaches and soothe the nerves. The oil is excellent for burns, chilblains, and insect bites in particular.

Lavender Sugar

Sprinkle lavender sugar over fruit salads, use it to make ice creams and other desserts, add it to cake batters, or whip it into cream-cheese frostings.

1 cup sugar
4 lavender spikes with flowers open, stems removed

Put the sugar into a screw-topped jar. Bruise the lavender spikes and bury them in the sugar. Cover tightly and leave for 2 weeks, shaking the jar every day. The sugar will then be ready for use, and will keep for up to one month.

Lavender Water

Put a quart of water to every pint of lavender picked from the stalk. Put them in a cold still over a slow fire. Distill very slowly, and put it into a pot till you have distilled the whole. Then clean your still well out, put your lavender water into it, and distill it off as slowly as before. Then put it into bottles, cork them quite close, and set them by for use.

FROM THE RECEIPT BOOK OF SUSANNAH STACEY,
QUOTED IN MARCUS WOODWARD,
THE MISTRESS OF STANTON'S FARM, 1938

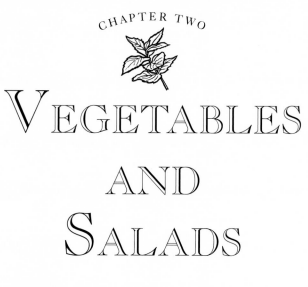

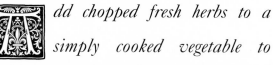

CHAPTER TWO

VEGETABLES
AND
SALADS

dd chopped fresh herbs to a simply cooked vegetable to transform its appearance and flavor. Whether you are boiling, steaming, or stir-frying vegetables, producing purées or summer salads, a sprinkling of herbs will make every vegetable dish special.

VEGETABLES AND SALADS

All vegetables, whether raw or cooked, can benefit from the addition of chopped fresh herbs. For cooked vegetables, the easiest approach is to toss the vegetables in herbs and melted butter just before serving. Try lemon thyme and fennel with spring greens; or use sour cream in place of butter, and add it with chervil to baby carrots. Another way to include herbs after cooking is to stir them into a creamy vegetable purée. Seasoning the vegetables with herbs during cooking also produces an excellent range of flavors. Simmer peas and lettuce with parsley and chervil, or cannelloni and pinto beans with thyme and marjoram.

The most flavorsome salads can be created with a mixture of unusual herbs, freshly picked from the garden. Try a combination of avocado and wild mushrooms, mixed in a basil and lemon dressing and spooned over peppery-flavored arugula leaves and crispy croutons. Use bulgar wheat with parsley and mint to make an authentic Middle Eastern tabbouleh; or reproduce the flavors of Greece with tomatoes, onion, olives, feta cheese, and oregano.

Majoram harvesting, Tacuinum Sanitatum manuscript, c. 1385.

PEAS *with* LETTUCE, PARSLEY, *and* CHERVIL

This is a typically French way of serving peas. Parsley and chervil are both very aromatic herbs and make this dish a light accompaniment, suited to most meat and fish dishes.

SERVES 4

1½ cups shelled peas
1 small lettuce, or 2½ cups
  shredded lettuce leaves
4 green onions, chopped
2tbsp chopped fresh parsley

2tbsp chopped fresh chervil
1tsp salt
1tsp sugar
2tbsp butter

Put all the ingredients in a saucepan, add 3 tablespoons water, and mix well. Bring to a boil, then turn down the heat and leave to simmer, covered, for 15 minutes. There should be very little liquid left in the pan at the end of cooking. Serve the peas with any juices that are left.

Companion Planting

Herbs can be beneficial to other plants growing near them, chiefly by keeping away insect pests with their strong scents. For this reason, herbs are sometimes planted in the vegetable garden or among flowers. Some aromatic plants, such as sage, marjoram, hyssop, and thyme, generally improve the health of the soil and of other plants growing around them. Why this happens,

however, has not been scientifically proved.
Herbs to plant near carrots to deter carrot fly: garlic, chives, pennyroyal, nasturtium, sage, rosemary, southernwood.
Herbs to repel whitefly: nasturtium, French marigold.
Herbs to plant near cabbages: nasturtium, sage, mint.
Herbs to plant near tomatoes: French marigold, basil.

HERBED-FRIED ZUCCHINI

This dish is suitable for serving with most meat and fish recipes. The zucchini slices are coated in a herb and flour mixture and then fried in butter. Using a plastic bag to coat the zucchini in the flour prevents the flour from making a mess everywhere.

SERVES 4

2tbsp all-purpose flour	*3 zucchini, weighing about*
1tsp salt	*14oz each, cut into*
Freshly ground black pepper	*½-inch slices*
3tbsp chopped fresh mixed	*2tsp vegetable oil*
herbs, such as parsley,	*3tbsp butter*
thyme, and oregano	

Combine the flour, salt, pepper, and herbs in a plastic bag. Add the zucchini slices. Then, holding the bag by the top to seal it, shake the zucchini until they are all coated in the herby flour.

Heat the butter and oil in a large skillet. Once the butter has melted, add the coated zucchini slices and sauté them for 3 minutes on each side, until they are golden brown. Remove from the pan and serve immediately.

THYME-ROASTED POTATOES

Roast potatoes are loved by nearly everyone and these delicious thyme-flavored ones are ideal to serve with roast meats and other vegetables. Try giving the same treatment to parsnips: they are equally scrumptious!

SERVES 4

1½lb potatoes	*6 fresh thyme sprigs*
6tbsp olive oil	

Preheat the oven to 375°F. Peel the potatoes and cut them into chunks. Put the chunks into boiling, salted water, and cook for 5 minutes, then drain.

Pour the oil into a shallow roasting pan and heat it in the preheated oven for 3 to 4 minutes. Tip the potatoes and the thyme into the hot oil, stirring the potatoes to coat them with oil. Roast for 50 to 60 minutes, turning the potatoes occasionally, so they are evenly browned and flavored with thyme.

BABY NEW CARROTS *with* SOUR CREAM *and* CHERVIL

Tender young carrots have a delicious, sweet flavor, which combines well with the slightly aniseed flavor of chervil. This is an ideal dish for serving during the summer, when carrots are at their sweetest. If chervil is unavailable, parsley is a good alternative.

SERVES 4

12oz baby new carrots
1tsp sugar
7tbsp sour cream or crème fraîche

3tbsp minced chervil or flat-leaf parsley
Salt and freshly ground black pepper

To prepare the carrots, simply rinse them under cold water, brushing off any dirt, and then top and tail them. Peel them if preferred, although this is not essential with baby carrots. Put the carrots in a saucepan with 4 tablespoons water and the sugar. Cover the pan with foil and then the lid and leave to simmer for 5 minutes, or until the carrots are tender.

Remove from the heat and drain off any excess water. Return the carrots to a very low heat and stir in the sour cream or crème fraîche, chervil or parsley, and seasoning. Simmer for 2 minutes, until the sour cream has melted and is heated through. Transfer to a warmed serving dish and serve immediately.

TABBOULEH *with* PARSLEY *and* MINT

This is a traditional dish in the Middle East. Masses of parsley, mint, and lemon juice give it a very refreshing taste and a real zing. Serve it as part of a selection of appetizers, on its own as a salad, or with pita bread as a light lunch.

SERVES 4

1 cup bulgar wheat (cracked
    wheat)
1 red onion, minced
1½ cups seeded and diced
    tomatoes
½ cup olive oil

¼ cup lemon juice
5tbsp minced fresh flat-leaf
    parsley
2tbsp minced fresh mint
Salt and freshly ground black
    pepper

Rinse the bulgar wheat under cold running water, then place in a large saucepan and cover with 2½ cups water. Bring to a boil. Reduce the heat, cover, and simmer for 10 to 15 minutes, until the wheat is tender and the water has been absorbed. Drain the wheat well, then fluff with a fork to separate the grains. Transfer to a large bowl.

Stir in the onion, tomatoes, olive oil, lemon juice, herbs, and seasoning, mix well and allow to cool to room temperature. This dish can be prepared up to one day in advance; simply combine all the ingredients, cover and chill.

Herb Recipes from Around the World

Many countries are renowned for certain recipes. Make American country-style chicken pie, Mexican salsa, or Russian lobio to sample authentic flavors from all around the world.

Sage is one of the most popular culinary herbs in the Southwest.

Dill pickles are frequently made in Eastern Europe, and dill is essential in the preparation of Gravad Lax, marinated salmon from Scandinavia.

U.S.A.
COUNTRY-STYLE CHICKEN PIE
A pie made from chicken poached with vegetables and 6 parsley sprigs for flavor, with large pieces of cooled and boned meat. It is placed in a baking dish lined with rich piecrust, coated in sauce made from the poaching stock and cream, then the chicken pieces are covered with more dough and baked.

CANADA
STUFFED BREAM BAKED IN RED WINE
Stuff bream with a mixture of bread crumbs, parsley, red bell pepper, egg yolk, and lemon juice, put into a dish with a mixture of red wine and crushed garlic and baked.

MEXICO
SALSA MEXICANA
A sauce to serve with tortillas made by combining peeled and chopped tomatoes, a chopped chili pepper, chopped onion, salt, and chopped cilantro leaves. Cilantro is a herb similar to coriander, which is used in Mexico, China, and Southeast Asia, as well as the Southwest.

GREAT BRITAIN
SAGE-AND-ONION STUFFING
A mixture of onions softened in butter, bread crumbs, salt, pepper, and sage, moistened with stock, milk, or cider. It is used for pork and poultry, particularly goose.

SCANDINAVIA
GRAVAD LAX
Fresh salmon, marinated for at least 48 hours with dill, salt, sugar, and crushed peppercorns. It is served raw with lemon wedges and mustard sauce.

GERMANY
RINDFLEISCH MIT SCHNITTLAUCHSOSSE (BOILED BEEF WITH CHIVE SAUCE)
A joint of beef boiled with vegetables and parsley sprigs, served with a sauce made from the thickened cooking liquid flavored with snipped chives and freshly grated nutmeg.

Nutmeg is classed as a spice rather than a herb. In its dried form it is often added to savory dishes with fresh herbs.

FRANCE
POULET À L'ESTRAGON (CHICKEN WITH TARRAGON)
A chicken stuffed with several tablespoons of butter beaten with tarragon, garlic, salt, and pepper, and with tarragon sprigs laid over the breast. It is roasted, basted with olive oil, then flamed in brandy. The juices are enriched with cream.

SPAIN
HABAS A LA CATALANA (FAVA BEANS WITH SAUSAGES AND MINT)
Fava beans are cooked with diced chorizo sausage and salt pork, green onions, a bay leaf, and chopped fresh mint.

ITALY
PESTO
A sauce for pasta which is made by pounding together fresh basil leaves, pine nuts, and garlic, and mixing the paste with Parmesan and Pecorino cheeses and either olive oil or a little softened butter.

GREECE
ARNI PSITO (ROAST LAMB)
A leg or shoulder of lamb is prepared by having slits cut into the skin and rosemary leaves and slivers of garlic pushed into them. It is put into a roasting pan and surrounded by sliced potatoes. Olive oil, water, and lemon juice are poured over the potatoes, which are then topped with a generous sprinkling of chopped oregano. The lamb is roasted until tender, the water absorbed, and the potatoes browned.

EASTERN EUROPE
DILL CUCUMBERS
Small cucumbers pickled in distilled vinegar with sprigs of dill and dill seeds to give them a distinctive flavor.

RUSSIAN FEDERATION
LOBIO
A dish of red kidney beans from the Caucasus. The cooked beans are mixed with a dressing of oil, white-wine vinegar, minced onion, and a blend of chopped parsley and cilantro. It is served cold as a salad.

SOUTH AFRICA
JUGGED VENISON
This traditional dish contains diced venison stewed with onions, celery, and lemon juice, and flavored with a bouquet garni of bay leaves, parsley, peppercorns, and cloves.

MIDDLE EAST
TZVAZEGH
These are small omelets flavored with mint and parsley, and served either as a first course or as a snack in warm pita breads. They are traditionally eaten at Easter.

INDIA
CILANTRO AND MINT CHUTNEY
A hot, green relish made by puréeing fresh cilantro and mint with a green chili, fresh gingerroot, and lemon juice.

CHINA
STIR-FRIED DISHES
The most-frequently used herb in Chinese cooking is garlic. For many stir-fried dishes it is crushed and sautéed in peanut oil with grated fresh gingerroot and chopped green onions before the main ingredients are added.

SOUTHEAST ASIA
GULAI TUMIS (SOUR FISH CURRY)
In this dish from Malaysia, dried chilies, lemon grass, browned onions, garlic, and spices are minced together to a fine paste and then sautéed in oil. Green beans and tamarind water are added, and then fish steaks.

It is always useful to have your own dried herbs hanging up in the kitchen. Here are bay, rosemary, sage, and thyme.

65

For a good, year-round supply of fresh herbs, grow your own. If you do not have a large space in the garden, they grow successfully in pots.

Avocado, Wild Mushroom, *and* Arugula Salad *with* Italian Dressing

This is an adventurous salad, perfect as a dinner-party appetizer. Peppery arugula leaves are combined with the delicate flavors of wild mushrooms, then tossed in an Italian dressing and piled onto toasted French bread. Serve this dish as soon after preparing as possible.

SERVES 4

½ French loaf, about 8 inches
    long
1 garlic clove, halved
3tbsp olive oil
1 ripe avocado, halved, peeled,
    and sliced
4oz wild mushrooms, such as
    chanterelle and porcini
2oz arugula leaves

DRESSING
5tbsp extra-virgin olive oil
1tbsp balsamic vinegar
1tsp lemon juice
6 fresh basil leaves, finely torn
Salt and freshly ground black
    pepper

Preheat the broiler to high. Cut the French loaf into 8 thin slices, on the diagonal, and rub each with garlic on both sides. Put on a baking tray and drizzle with 2 tablespoons of the oil. Place under the hot broiler and broil for 2 to 3 minutes on both sides, until golden brown and toasted.

Meanwhile, heat the remaining tablespoon of oil in a skillet and gently sauté the wild mushrooms for about 5 minutes. Transfer to a plate to cool slightly.

Combine the dressing ingredients in a screw-top jar and shake well. Put the arugula leaves in a bowl and pour half the dressing over. Toss the leaves well. Put 2 slices of bread on each plate, divide the arugula leaves between them and top with slices of avocado and the wild mushrooms. Pour the remaining dressing over and serve.

Alternatively, put the arugula, avocado, and wild mushrooms in a large bowl, pour the dressing over, and toss well. Arrange the slices of French bread around the edge of the bowl and serve as soon as possible.

Shredded Cabbage *and* Green Greens *with* Fennel *and* Balm

Balm is a very fast-growing herb, and this recipe is a good way of making use of it. This dish makes an ideal accompaniment to roasts.

SERVES 4

Pinch of salt
5½ cups shredded white
    cabbage
5½ cups shredded spring greens
2tbsp butter, diced

1tsp fennel seeds, or 1tbsp
    minced feathery fronds from
    fresh fennel
4tbsp roughly chopped fresh
    balm
Freshly ground black pepper

Place ⅔ cup water and a pinch of salt in a large saucepan and bring to a boil. Add the cabbage and spring greens and simmer for 10 minutes, until most of the water has evaporated but the cabbage is still fairly crisp. Increase the heat, to evaporate any remaining liquid. Add the butter, fennel, balm, and pepper to the pan and stir until the butter melts. Toss the vegetables in the butter and herbs and transfer to a warmed serving dish. Serve immediately.

WINTER BEANS *with* THYME, MARJORAM, *and* PARSLEY

This recipe suggests using cannellini and pinto beans, but almost any combination of canned beans can be used. The beans are simmered in a delicious tomato and mixed herb stew. Serve as an accompaniment to meat and poultry dishes, or with boiled rice and crusty bread for a complete vegetarian meal.

SERVES 4

1 cup canned cannellini beans
1 cup canned pinto beans
2tbsp vegetable oil
1 large onion, halved and sliced
1 fat garlic clove, crushed
1¾ cups fresh or canned tomatoes, chopped

1tbsp chopped fresh thyme leaves
2tbsp minced fresh marjoram
4tbsp minced fresh parsley
1tbsp soy sauce
Salt and freshly ground black pepper

Rinse the beans under cold running water and drain them well. Set aside.

Heat the oil in a large saucepan and gently fry the onion for 10 minutes, until softened. Stir in the garlic and fry for 1 minute longer. Add the tomatoes, thyme, marjoram, and 1 tablespoon of the parsley. Stir well and bring to a boil. Reduce the heat and simmer for 10 minutes. Stir in the beans, soy sauce, and seasoning and simmer for 5 to 10 minutes longer, until the beans are heated through. Remove from the heat and stir in the remaining parsley. Serve immediately.

68

HERB SALAD

Some herb leaves are more commonly associated with the garden than the kitchen. Leaves such as dandelion and nasturtium, however, are edible as long as they have not been contaminated with pesticides or traffic fumes, of course, and make an unusual talking point at dinner. Pick undamaged, young leaves and wash them well before using. Leaves such as dandelion are rich in vitamin A, calcium, and iron, and are very nutritious.

Place all the salad leaves and sprigs of herbs in a bowl and stir them together. Combine the olive oil, balsamic vinegar, and seasoning in a screw-top jar and shake to combine them thoroughly.

Just before serving, pour the dressing over the salad leaves and toss well. Scatter the edible flowers over the top and serve immediately.

SERVES 4

2oz mixed herb leaves, such as dandelion, nasturtium, and red mustard
3oz arugula leaves
1 lettuce heart, each leaf torn in three
10 sprigs fresh flat-leaf parsley, cilantro, and/or chervil

DRESSING
4tbsp olive oil
1tbsp balsamic vinegar
Salt and freshly ground black pepper

TO SERVE
Borage, nasturtium, or other edible flowers

69

GREEK SALAD *with* OREGANO DRESSING

One of the best things about a vacation in Greece is the first taste of an authentic Greek salad, made with salty feta cheese, plump olives, and rich olive oil, eaten with the sun beating down. Re-create the taste of Greece with this salad below, which is tossed in an oregano dressing.

SERVES 4

1 small red onion, sliced
6oz feta cheese, cubed
20 black olives
1 small green bell pepper, seeded and sliced
4 small ripe tomatoes, or 1 large beefsteak tomato, roughly chopped

DRESSING
3tbsp olive oil, preferably extra-virgin
1tbsp lemon juice
2 tbsp minced fresh oregano
Freshly ground black pepper

TO SERVE (OPTIONAL)
Lettuce or salad leaves
Cubed cucumber

Put the onion, feta cheese, olives, green bell pepper, and tomatoes in a bowl and mix well. Put the dressing ingredients in a screw-top jar and shake. Pour the dressing over the salad and toss. If you like, serve the Greek salad on a bed of salad leaves and cucumber.

CARROT *and* CILANTRO PUREE

This quick vegetable purée makes a flavorful alternative to boiled carrots with roast meat.

SERVES 4

4¹/₂ cup carrots cut into ¹/₂-inch slices
4tbsp roughly chopped fresh cilantro leaves

3tbsp light cream
Fresh cilantro sprigs, to garnish

Put the sliced carrots in a medium-size saucepan and just cover them with water. Cover and bring to a boil. Lower the heat and leave to simmer for 15 minutes, or until the carrots are very tender. Drain well. Put the carrots in a food processor with the chopped cilantro and cream and process to a smooth purée. Or, push the carrots through a strainer or food mill and stir in the chopped cilantro.

Return the carrots to a clean pan and gently heat through. Serve garnished with cilantro sprigs.

Galen, c. A.D. 130–200

Claudius Galen was born in Pergamon in Asia Minor and moved to Alexandria to study at its famous medical school and later to practice medicine.
Galen became famous for treating gladiators after their skirmishes in the arena. He acquired such a distinguished reputation that when he went to Rome, he was invited to become the personal physician of the emperor Marcus Aurelius. When the emperor died in A.D. 180, Galen kept his position and was physician to succeeding emperors until his own death.
Galen believed all disease arose from the imbalance of the body's four humors: blood, bile, phlegm, and choler.
He chose all his plant remedies in relation to these, rating them on a four-point scale, saying, for example, "This plant is hot and moist in the third degree." From him came the term "simple," meaning a herb possessing a single quality, such as heat.
Not long after Galen's death, the Roman Empire collapsed, removing the likelihood of any early challenge to his views. In fact, his ideas were not completely overturned until the end of the 17th century.

71

Native American Medicine

The medicine that was practiced by Native Americans in the 17th century involved the use of herbs that were new to the British colonists, but many were soon included in the list of standard household remedies, and are still being used today.

This etching shows the lodge of a Midiwine holy man during an initiation ceremony. The initiate, as he passed from lodge to lodge, learned more of the medicinal qualities of certain herbs.

When the first settlers left England to settle in Plymouth and Boston, the native Americans they encountered were fit and strong. They lived mainly outdoors, eating a diet of fresh wild meat, raw fruit and vegetables, whole grains, nuts, and unpolluted spring water. Alcohol was virtually unknown to them and the smoking of tobacco had a ritual purpose rather than being a regular part of daily life. They felt at one with their surroundings and they had an intimate knowledge of the plants that they found in their immediate vicinity.

When they were ill, their cures were almost always herbal. Parasitic diseases, such as worms, were the most common, so there were many herbal emetics and purges. After the cause of the disease had been expelled, healing herbal decoctions (essences extracted by boiling) were administered while the patient

The scalp dance, as it was recorded by George Caitlin in 1844.

fasted. The fast was followed by a light, vegetarian diet until good health had been restored.

Internal remedies tended to be specific —using a single herb for a particular illness. Many were boiled as a decoction; others were steeped for a long time in cold water. In addition to the leafy parts of plants, the Native Americans also used roots and barks, which were dried and then crushed between flat stones. Oils were extracted from nuts, and ointments were made with animal fat.

One herb that the settlers found useful was *Eupatorium perfoliatum*, which became known as boneset. All the Indian tribes used it to treat fevers and chills, and boneset tea became a common settlers' tonic for malaria, influenza, and typhoid.

Other herbal applications were not shared between tribes, and in some cases the same herb was used for a range of different treatments. The herb blue flag (*Iris versicolor*), for example, was used as an emetic by the Ojibwa, as a poultice for leg ulcers by the Albany Indians, and as a decoction for colds and chest ailments by the Meskwakis.

The Native Americans knew that sometimes body and mind had to be cured together, and healing rituals that involved chanting and drumming united the force of the whole tribe in treating a patient. One of the most widely practiced combined treatments for mental and physical health was the ritual cleansing that took place in the sweat lodge. This was a religious experience as well as a healing process, and in some cases it served as an initiation rite. Sweat lodges took a number of forms. In the northeast, they consisted of wooden frames covered with birch bark or animal skins. In the southeast, they were earth mounds dug into a hillside beside a stream; and in the northwest, they were made of cedar planks. They were often heated by hot stones,

sometimes sprinkled with aromatic herbs. Within this small shelter, the patient, spiritual seeker, or initiate would sweat out the impurities of body and mind.

At the beginning of the 20th century, Native American knowledge and traditions were in danger of being stamped out and forgotten. Today, they are undergoing a revival as their values are being recognized.

The shaman, or medicine man, used drumming, dance, and chanting as part of his cures. Herbs were also an essential part of the healing process.

73

CHAPTER THREE

MEAT AND POULTRY

ake one basic meat ingredient, and you can produce a whole variety of different dishes simply by changing the herbs used to flavor it. And with the wide selection of meats, poultry, and herbs available, you have endless choice of style and flavor.

MEAT AND POULTRY

Certain classic dishes are always associated with particular combinations of herbs. One of these is beef en croûte, in which a beef tenderloin is encased in pastry with onions, parsley, oregano, thyme, and sage. Lamb and mint are another time-honored partnership, and a mint and yogurt sauce is particularly good with broiled lamb chops. Sage and onion stuffing is the traditional accompaniment to roast pork; but marjoram also works well either with pork cooked in cream and cider or mixed with parsley and thyme to flavor succulent homemade pork sausages. One of the most versatile meats is chicken. Pot roast it with vegetables and a bouquet garni for a farmhouse-style dinner. For a light, healthy meal, slowly bake chicken breasts in a foil package with fresh ginger, soy sauce, chives, and tarragon; or make an authentic Thai curry, flavored with lemongrass. For a very special meal, stuff quail with a mixture of goat cheese and tarragon, and broil with herbes de Provence.

Pig killing in December, as illustrated in the Breviary of Henry 1 of Este *(a book of psalms, hymns, and prayers), 15th-century manusript.*

BEEF EN CROUTE *with* HERBS *and* RED WINE SAUCE

This is a delicious treat for serving at Sunday lunch or at a dinner party. Buy the thick end of the tenderloin for this dish. Although dried herbs can be substituted, fresh ones make all the difference.

SERVES 4

1tbsp sunflower oil
2tbsp butter
1¼lb beef tenderloin (thick end)
2 onions, minced
1tbsp minced fresh parsley
1tbsp minced fresh oregano
1tbsp minced fresh thyme
1tbsp minced fresh sage
9oz puff pastry dough,
  defrosted if frozen

1 small egg, beaten
Salt and freshly ground black
  pepper

SAUCE
1tbsp all-purpose flour
1¼ cups red wine
1¼ cups beef stock

Preheat the oven to 425°F. Heat the oil and butter in a skillet and fry the beef until it is browned all over. Remove the beef from the pan and leave it to cool. Fry the onions in the same pan, with any fat or juices left from the beef, for 10 minutes, until soft and golden. Use a slotted spoon to transfer the onions to a bowl, leaving any fat in the pan. Stir the herbs into the onions and season well.

Roll out the dough on a lightly floured work surface, to a size large enough to encase the beef. Spoon three-quarters of the onion and herb mixture over the dough, leaving a 2-inch border all around the edge. Put the beef in the middle of the dough and spread the remaining onion mixture over the top. Enclose the beef in the dough, sealing the edge with beaten egg and trimming off any excess dough. Place the package on a greased baking sheet, seal-side down. Using any trimmings, cut out leaves or make other decorations. Brush the whole surface with more beaten egg, add any decorations and brush these with beaten egg. Make a small hole in the middle of the dough to allow steam to escape. Bake for 40 minutes for rare beef, 50 to 55 minutes for medium beef, and 60 to 80 minutes for well-done beef.

Meanwhile, make the sauce. Stir the flour into the pan juices and cook for 1 minute. Gradually add the wine and stock, stirring to remove any lumps, and bring to a boil. Season well, reduce the heat, and simmer for 5 to 10 minutes, until the sauce is reduced slightly. Strain into a gravy boat.

To serve, carefully transfer the beef to a warmed serving dish, without breaking the pastry. Carve it into slices at the table, and serve accompanied by the red wine sauce.

BROILED QUAIL STUFFED *with* TARRAGON

Although this dish is a little fiddly to prepare, it is well worth the effort for an elegant dinner. The birds are stuffed under their skin with a mixture of tarragon, goat cheese, and mushrooms. They can be prepared in advance and kept refrigerated until you cook them. Serve accompanied by sautéed potatoes and green vegetables.

SERVES 4

4 quail, dressed
2tsp dried herbes de
  Provence—thyme, summer
  savory, lavender, and
  rosemary (optional)
Salt and freshly ground black
  pepper

STUFFING
2tbsp olive oil
1½ cups very finely chopped
  button mushrooms
1 fat garlic clove, crushed
3oz soft goat cheese
3 to 4tbsp finely chopped fresh
  tarragon

First prepare the stuffing. Heat 1 tablespoon of the oil in a skillet and gently fry the mushrooms, uncovered, for 4 to 5 minutes, until most of the liquid in the pan has evaporated. Stir in the garlic for the last minute. Remove the pan from the heat and let the mushrooms cool in the pan for about 10 minutes. Stir in the goat cheese, tarragon, and seasoning, mix to a smooth consistency, and leave to cool completely.

To prepare each quail, put the quail breast-side down and, using poultry shears, cut along both sides of the backbone, to split open the bird; discard the backbone. Open the bird out and turn it over breast-side up. Press down with the heel of your hand to break the breastbone and rib cage and flatten out the bird. From the neck end, carefully separate the breast skin from the flesh. Divide the stuffing into quarters and then, using your fingers, carefully push the stuffing under the skin of each bird, smoothing the surface of each bird once it is stuffed. Fold the skin over the opening to seal. Using a small knife, make a slit in the skin between the legs and then bend and tuck the legs through the slit, to keep the bird in a neat shape.

Preheat the broiler to high. Rub each bird with the remaining olive oil and sprinkle the *herbes de Provence* over (if using). Broil, breast-side down, for about 20 minutes. Turn the birds over and broil them for 10 minutes longer. Depending on how well done you want the meat, cook the quail for a slightly longer or shorter period of time.

The Physicians of Myddfai, 13th century

The physicians of Myddfai in Wales were said to have been founded by Rhiwallon, the legendary son of the magical lady from the Lake of Llyn y Van Vach and a local farmer. When the lady returned to her lake she is said to have passed the knowledge of healing herbs to Rhiwallon, who formed the order of the physicians of Myddfai with his three sons.

Members of the order served as personal physicians to the Princes of South Wales for nearly 1,000 years, ending in the 19th century when the last of the line was buried. At the beginning of the 13th century, their lord of the manor, Rys Gryg, encouraged them to record their knowledge for posterity.

The physicians used what we would now call a holistic approach to medicine, emphasising each patient's responsibility for his or her own health and treating the causes of the disease as well as the symptoms. In devising a cure the health of the patient's whole body was looked at, as well as his or her state of mind. Their writings not only give herbal cures but also philosophies of healthy living, such as: "The bread of yesterday, the meat of today, and the wine of last year will produce health."

They had at their disposal about 900 herbs, mainly those that grew prolifically in their area, both wild and cultivated in garden plots. They specified the parts to use and the amounts, as well as the need for such things as clean water for their infusions, decoctions, and poultices. Theirs was a sensible, simple medicine that would not be out of place today.

LAMB *with* YOGURT *and* MINT SAUCE

Lamb is traditionally served with mint and this recipe uses mint with a refreshing yogurt sauce. This dish tastes wonderful accompanied by small new potatoes and a vegetable or two, or a salad.

SERVES 4

2 racks of lamb, each with 6 or
   7 cutlets
1tbsp olive or vegetable oil

SAUCE
1tbsp olive or vegetable oil
²⁄₃ cup plain yogurt
3tbsp minced fresh mint
Pinch of salt and white pepper

First make the sauce. Combine all the ingredients together in a bowl and leave the flavors to develop while you prepare the lamb.

   Preheat the oven to 375°F. Slice any skin and most fat off the racks of lamb, leaving a thin, even layer of fat. Score the fat with diagonal cuts in a diamond pattern and season with salt and pepper. Roast for 25 to 30 minutes for slightly pink meat or for 5 to 10 minutes longer for medium to well-done meat.

   Carve the racks of lamb into individual chops and serve with the yogurt and mint sauce.

DUCK BREASTS *with* ORANGE *and* MINT

Canard à l'orange is probably one of the most famous recipes for duck and fruit. This recipe is a variation on the theme, with the addition of mint, which goes surprisingly well with orange. Serve the duck with sautéed or roast potatoes and green beans.

SERVES 4

3 oranges
3 large duck breast halves
   (with the skin on), cut into
   large pieces
1tbsp olive oil
1tbsp all-purpose flour
1¼ cups good-quality duck or
   chicken stock

1tbsp brown sugar
4 or 5tbsp mint leaves,
   shredded
Salt and freshly ground black
   pepper
3tbsp port wine

Thinly peel the zest (not the pith) from 2 of the oranges and cut it into thin strips. Then remove all the pith and segment the oranges. Blanch the strips of orange zest in boiling water for 5 minutes, then drain and set them aside. Squeeze the juice from the remaining orange and set it aside.

   Heat the olive oil in a large skillet over high heat and fry the duck breasts until thoroughly browned on all sides. Remove the duck from the pan and keep warm. Remove all but 1 tablespoon of fat from the pan, sprinkle in the flour and mix to form a paste. Cook for a couple of minutes, stirring frequently to scrape up any bits left in the pan. Gradually pour in the stock, stirring to form a smooth sauce, then stir in the sugar, orange juice, and peel and season with salt and pepper. Bring to a boil, reduce the heat, and add the pieces of duck. Simmer for 5 minutes longer, adding the mint leaves and orange segments for the final 2 minutes. Check the seasoning and stir in the port wine. Serve immediately.

THAI CHICKEN CURRY *with* CILANTRO *and* LEMONGRASS

Thai curries have very thin sauces, compared to Indian curries, so provide plenty of boiled rice to mop up the sauce.

SERVES 4

1-inch piece fresh gingerroot, peeled and chopped	1tsp salt
3 fresh red chilies, seeded and roughly chopped	1tbsp vegetable oil
2 garlic cloves, chopped	4 skinless, boneless chicken breast halves, shredded
2 shallots, chopped	13-oz can of coconut milk
2-inch piece lemongrass, finely chopped	7½-ounce can of bamboo shoots
2tsp coriander seeds	1 cup quartered button mushrooms
	3 to 4tbsp fresh cilantro leaves

In a mortar and pestle (or a coffee grinder if you keep one solely for spices), grind together the ginger, chilies, garlic, shallots, lemongrass, coriander seeds, and salt to a paste. If you do not have either, put the ingredients in a small bowl and use the end of a rolling pin to crush everything.

Heat the oil over a high heat in a skillet or wok and fry the paste for 30 seconds. Add the shredded chicken and stir-fry for 2 minutes. Pour in the coconut milk and bring to a boil, then reduce the heat, cover the pan, and leave to simmer for 10 minutes. Add the bamboo shoots and mushrooms and simmer for 2 minutes longer.

Remove the pan from the heat, stir in the cilantro leaves, and serve, accompanied by boiled rice.

81

Herbs in a Monastery Garden

Imagine peace and stillness, the humming of bees, bird song, the sound of a trickling fountain and, wafting through the air, the aromatic scent of herbs. Herb gardens in monasteries all over Europe from the 9th to 15th centuries were very much like this.

A selection of different thymes that would have been grown in a monastery garden. They were useful in the kitchen and also in the infirmary where they were made into remedies for coughs and colds.

Herbs were important in monastic life. They enlivened the plain daily meals in the refectory; they provided medicines for the monks and for the local villagers; they were strewn on the floor of the abbey, giving out a sweet scent as they were crushed underfoot; and they helped to keep living and sleeping quarters free of insect pests. The herb garden itself was a place of calm and solace, where the monks could sit and contemplate beneath arbors of bay or honeysuckle.

A list of useful herbs, both medicinal and culinary, was drawn up in the 9th century by Charlemagne, King of the Franks and Emperor of the Holy Roman Empire, advised by Alcuin, an English monk who had become abbot of the monastery of St. Martin at Tours in France. Soon afterward, Walafrid Strabo, a monk at the island monastery of Reichenau in Switzerland, wrote a list of the 29 plants he considered the most valuable. Between them, these lists had a great influence on monastery gardens until the time of the Reformation in the 16th century.

The monastery garden was often described as the *hortus conclusus* (enclosed garden) because it was surrounded by a wattle fence about 4 feet tall. This was made in spring, when the young shoots of hazel and willow were supple. Stakes were driven into the ground around the garden and the shoots were woven between them. The fence kept out animals, such as deer and rabbits, and any human thieves who wanted to help themselves to the monastery's herbs and vegetables. It also gave a sense of peace and privacy.

One monk, often called the herberer, was in charge of the herb garden, and he had a team of helpers, usually sturdy young novices, to do the digging. Gardening was the same for a medieval monk as it is for a herb gardener today: in the spring there would be sowing and

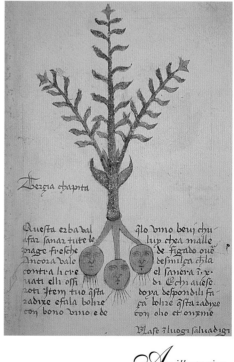

An illustration from a 14th-century Italian herbal.

Medieval monks weeding in the monastery garden.

82

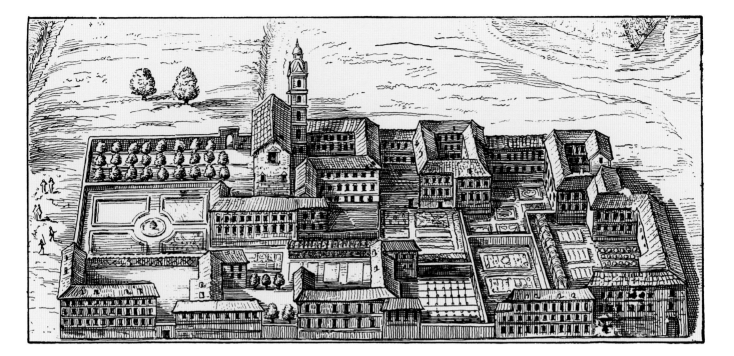

planting out; in the summer, weeding, trimming, and harvesting; and in the fall the final cutting back, digging, and preparation for winter.

Once the herbs were harvested, they were taken to the herbarium, also the province of the herberer, where they were hung up in bunches to dry. Herbs such as fennel or poppy were suspended with their seed heads in linen bags, so, after a good shaking, the seeds could drop into the bag and could be saved. Some of the seeds were set aside for culinary or medicinal use, others were stored for sowing the following spring.

The herberer had a wide knowledge of the properties of his plants. He made the various ointments, liniments, and medicines that the infirmarer, in charge of the hospital, required. These preparations included garlic, hore-hound, thyme and angelica, and elecampane for coughs and colds; sage and mallow for sore throats; fennel and mint for digestive prob-lems; balm, chamomile, and borage to soothe and relax; marjoram and parsley for rheumatism; rue, cornflower, and clary sage for sore eyes; clover and yarrow for wounds and sores; and the opium poppy to dull severe pain. This last, because of its powerful effect and the danger of addiction if it fell into the wrong hands, may have been grown in a locked area of the garden, together with the other potentially hazardous plants, such as foxglove

used for heart problems and deadly nightshade used as a sedative.

In the kitchen, parsley, hyssop, savory, thyme, lovage, chives, and garlic improved the flavor of the thick bean or pea soup, known as *pottage*, which was the staple diet in most monasteries. Mint, parsley, fennel, and marj-oram went into sauces for fish, and the abbot's roast lamb needed thyme. Ale was flavored with alecost and bog myrtle, and bread with coriander seeds.

Southernwood, wormwood, and pennyroyal were the favorite insect repellents. Mullein stems were dipped in tallow to make candles. The stems formed a wick which burned with the wax. Rosemary was burned in a dish with other herbs or prec-ious ingredients, such as frankincense, and used as an incense.

Somewhere in the herb garden may have been a plot dedicated to the Virgin Mary, for many plants were associated with her. It could have contained woodruff, cow-slips, violets, lily of the valley, thyme, and penny-royal, and would have been an area of especially quiet reflection.

A view of a Turin monastery in 1682 showing the herb gardens on the right.

83

Sage was used for cleaning teeth and also as a cure for sore throats. In the abbot's kitchen, it was used to make rich meats more digestible.

HOMEMADE PORK *and* HERB SAUSAGES

Homemade sausages are fairly quick to make and children will love helping to shape them. Serve the sausages with mashed potatoes and gravy or bay leaf and oregano sauce (page 122). Chill any leftover sausages and eat them cold.

SERVES 4 (MAKES 8 SAUSAGES)

2tbsp oil
1 large onion, minced
1 fat garlic clove, crushed
13oz good-quality, lean ground pork, lamb, or beef
1 cup fresh bread crumbs
1 egg yolk

2tbsp minced fresh parsley
2tbsp minced fresh thyme
2tbsp minced fresh marjoram
Salt and freshly ground black pepper
Oil

Heat the oil in a pan and gently fry the onion for about 10 minutes, until softened. Stir in the garlic and fry for 1 minute. Remove the pan from the heat and allow the onions to cool. Combine the remaining ingredients (except the oil) in a bowl and stir in the onions. Mix well. Divide the mixture into 8 portions and shape each portion into a sausage shape, about 4 inches long. Chill in the refrigerator for 30 to 60 minutes.

These sausages are delicious baked, broiled, or fried. To bake them, preheat the oven to 375°F. Put the sausages in a greased baking dish and bake for 35 to 40 minutes. To broil them, preheat the broiler to high. Line the broiler pan with foil and brush the foil with oil. Broil the sausages for 10 to 12 minutes, turning them occasionally, until cooked through. To fry the sausages, heat 1 to 2 tablespoons of oil in a large skillet over medium heat and gently fry the sausages for 10 to 12 minutes, turning them once during cooking.

If you are making a gravy to serve with the sausages, make it in the same skillet and scrape up any bits of meat left in the pan to enrich it.

BAKED CHICKEN *with* CHIVES *and* TARRAGON

This dish is perfect both for a family supper and for a dinner party. Leave the chicken to marinate overnight and then put it into the oven. If you are running short of time, you don't even need to thicken the sauce: simply serve it straight from the baking dish. Serve with buttered noodles, rice or potatoes, and a green vegetable.

SERVES 4

4 skinless, boneless chicken breast halves
2-inch piece of fresh gingerroot, peeled and grated
1tbsp clear honey
1tbsp soy sauce
4tbsp dry white wine
2tbsp finely snipped fresh chives
2tbsp minced fresh tarragon
1tsp cornstarch

Make several deep incisions across the surface of each chicken piece. Put the remaining ingredients (except the cornstarch) in a small bowl and mix well. Place the chicken breast halves in a baking dish large enough to hold them in a single layer and pour the sauce over. Cover the dish with foil and leave to marinate in the refrigerator for at least 2 hours or overnight, turning once.

Preheat the oven to 375°F. Turn the chicken pieces once more and replace the foil. Bake for 30 minutes, until the chicken is tender and juices run clear when pierced with a skewer.

Transfer the chicken to a warmed serving dish and pour the cooking liquid into a small saucepan over high heat. Mix the cornstarch with 1 tablespoon cold water and add to the pan. Bring the sauce to a boil and cook for 2 to 3 minutes, until it has thickened slightly. Serve each chicken piece with a little of the sauce.

CHICKEN *and* VEGETABLES *in a* POT *with* BOUQUET GARNI

This dish should be made in a very large flameproof casserole. A bouquet garni of parsley sprigs, bay leaf, and thyme gives a subtle herb flavor to the gravy made from the cooking juices.

SERVES 4

3tbsp vegetable oil
4-ounce thick piece of smoked bacon, cut in ½-inch cubes
2 carrots, peeled and cut into 1-inch chunks
2 celery stalks, cut into 1-inch pieces
12 pearl onions, peeled but left whole
2 leeks, trimmed and cut into 1-inch pieces
1 garlic clove, crushed
3 to 4lb whole chicken (without giblets), rinsed and patted dry
1¼ cups chicken stock
1 cup dry white wine
Salt and freshly ground black pepper
3 or 4 fresh parsley sprigs, 1 fresh bay leaf, and 3 fresh thyme sprigs, tied into a bouquet garni
1½ cups quartered flat-cap mushrooms
1tbsp cornstarch, mixed with 1tbsp cold water
3 to 4tbsp light cream (optional)

Preheat the oven to 375°F. Heat 1 tablespoon of the oil over high heat in a large flameproof casserole. Add the bacon and fry until golden, stirring occasionally. Using a draining spoon, transfer it to a dish and set aside. Add the remaining 2 tablespoons of oil to the pan with the carrots, celery, onions, leeks, and garlic and fry until browned. Remove the vegetables and add them to the reserved bacon. Add the whole chicken to the pot and brown it on all sides. Then return the vegetables and bacon to the pan, pour the stock and wine over, season, and add the bouquet garni. Bring to a simmer, then cover the pot and bake for 1 hour, occasionally basting the chicken with the cooking juices.

Stir in the mushrooms and cook for 30 minutes longer. Uncover for the last 15 minutes to allow the breast to become crisp. Test if the chicken is cooked by inserting a skewer into the thigh; the chicken is cooked once the juices run clear. Transfer the cooked chicken to a warmed serving dish and cover with a dome of foil to keep warm. Remove the vegetables and keep warm. Discard the bouquet garni and put the casserole over high heat. Bring the cooking juices to a boil, add the cornstarch and stir until thickened. Check the seasoning, stir in the cream, if using, and pour into a warmed gravy boat.

To serve, arrange the vegetables around the chicken and serve the gravy separately.

USING HERBS AS FLAVORINGS

T he following recipes are quick and easy. These are ideal when you buy a whole packet of herbs when you only need 1 or 2 tablespoons, or you may have a glut of homegrown herbs. The recipes are, of course, good enough to justify buying herbs just to make them!

FLAVORED OILS

Flavored oils used to be made by gently crushing herbs and adding them to oil, which was then left for several weeks, if not months, before being used. However, the thinking nowadays is that you should heat herbs in the oil, so their flavor infuses into the oil, and then discard them, to prevent any bacteria present on the herbs from multiplying in the airless environment of the oil. Make small batches of flavored oils, keep them in the refrigerator, and use them within 1 to 2 days.

MAKES 6TBSP

6tbsp extra-virgin olive oil   *3tbsp fresh herbs, gently crushed*

Gently heat the oil in a small pan and add the crushed herbs. Simmer for 5 to 10 minutes to let the flavor of the herbs infuse into the oil. Leave the oil to cool, then strain into a suitable container, such as a glass bottle. Use the flavored oil as you would olive oil, such as for tossing pasta, for salad dressings, in mayonnaise, and for pan frying.

FLAVORED VINEGARS

To really enjoy the flavor of a herb vinegar, prepare it a couple of weeks in advance to make sure the flavor is sufficiently developed. Add a fresh sprig or two of the chosen herb at the final bottling stage, for ease of identification and for decoration. Herb vinegars make delightful presents and, with a little help from an adult, children can make them as gifts for relations. Use the flavored vinegar in salad dressings and sauces. Particularly popular herb vinegars are dill and tarragon but you can use almost any herb.

MAKES 1 QUART

1½oz chopped fresh herbs
1 quart white- or red-wine vinegar

Fresh herb sprigs, to garnish

Put the herbs in a glass container with a tightly fitting lid (or several containers) and pour the vinegar over. Cover and store in a dark place at room temperature for 1 to 2 weeks, gently shaking the bottle once a day. After this time, strain the liquid through a cheesecloth-lined strainer into pretty glass bottles. Add a fresh sprig or two of the herb used for flavoring. The vinegar will keep for several months in a cool, dark place. In sunlight, the sprig of herb will quickly lose its color.

HERB BUTTERS

Herb butters can be used in a multitude of ways, such as over hot pasta, on top of steaks, for making garlic bread, and for spreading on plain bread. Almost any herb can be used but basil, tarragon, chives, parsley, and cilantro are particularly delicious. Try combinations of herbs, such as parsley and chives, and chervil and tarragon.

MAKES ½ CUP

½ cup butter, at room temperature

3tbsp minced fresh herbs

Soften (but do not melt) the butter by beating it in a bowl with a wooden spoon. Stir in the herbs, mixing well. Lay a piece of plastic wrap on the countertop and spoon the butter onto the plastic in an oblong shape. Wrap the butter and roll it to form a fat tube, about 6 inches long. Place the butter in the refrigerator to harden. As and when required, unwrap it and cut it in slices.

Alternatively, spoon the butter into small ramekins, chill in the refrigerator, and serve from the ramekins at the table.

87

LOIN OF PORK *with* FRESH SAGE *and* ONION STUFFING

Sage is synonymous with stuffings and makes a traditional and good accompaniment to pork. Here, sage and onion stuffing is used to fill a boneless loin of pork, which is then roasted with strips of bacon.

SERVES 4 TO 6

1 boneless loin of pork tenderloin, weighing 2 to 2¹/₂lb	STUFFING
	1tbsp vegetable oil
Salt and freshly ground black pepper	1 large onion, minced
	4tbsp white bread crumbs, made from day-old bread
5 bacon slices	3tbsp minced fresh sage
1tbsp all-purpose flour	1 egg, beaten
1¹/₄ cups hard cider or apple juice	

Preheat the oven to 375°F. To make the stuffing, heat the oil in a skillet and gently fry the onion for about 10 minutes, or until softened. Leave the onion to cool slightly. Transfer to a bowl and stir in all the other stuffing ingredients.

Slice horizontally through the loin of pork, stopping about 1 inch from the second edge, so the meat can be opened out like a book. Open the meat, season it with salt and pepper and spread the stuffing over half. Replace the other half, arrange the bacon along the top of the meat, and tie the meat into a neat shape with kitchen string at 1-inch intervals.

Place the meat in a roasting pan and roast for 60 to 70 minutes. Transfer to a carving board and cover with a foil dome to allow the meat to rest while making the gravy.

Spoon off all but 1 tablespoon of the fat from the roasting pan and then put the pan over medium heat on the stovetop. Stir in the flour and mix with the bits left in the bottom of the pan. Gradually pour in the cider, stirring well to prevent lumps forming. Increase the heat and boil the gravy to thicken it slightly. Once it has thickened, transfer to a warmed gravy boat.

Carve the pork into thick slices and serve with the gravy.

PORK SCALLOPS *in a* CIDER, SWEET MARJORAM, *and* CREAM SAUCE *with* APPLE *and* POTATO MASH

Pork cooked in cider and cream is a traditional dish that is enhanced by the addition of sweet marjoram.

SERVES 4

4 boneless pork scallops	MASH
1tbsp butter	2 green eating apples, peeled, cored, and quartered
3 shallots, minced	
1¹/₄ cups hard cider	2¹/₂ cups peeled and chopped potatoes
5tbsp light cream	
3tbsp minced fresh sweet marjoram	2tbsp butter
	3tbsp milk
	Salt and freshly ground black pepper

First, put the apples and potatoes in a large saucepan and cover with water. Bring to a boil and simmer for about 20 minutes. Drain, return them to the pan and set aside with the lid on.

Put the pork scallops between 2 sheets of waxed paper and strike them gently with a meat mallet to flatten them to about ¹/₂ inch thick. Melt the butter in a skillet. Add the shallots and fry gently for 5 minutes, until softened. Add the scallops and fry them on both sides for about 3 minutes. Remove to a warmed plate and keep warm.

Pour in the cider, increase the heat, and boil rapidly until it has reduced by a quarter. Stir in the cream, seasoning, and marjoram. Return the scallops to the pan and heat them for 1 or 2 minutes. Meanwhile, put the pan with the potatoes and apples over medium heat and shake it to evaporate off any moisture. Mash the apple and potatoes with the butter and milk. Season well. Once the scallops are heated through, serve with the mash.

89

The Chelsea Physic Garden

Founded in 1673 by the Society of Apothecaries, the Chelsea Physic Garden, in London, has undergone periods of expansion and decline. It is now one of the best-known medicinal herb gardens in the world, and provides a green haven in the busy city, as well as a center for research into the healing properties of plants.

James I, who granted the charter to the Society of Apothecaries in 1617.

The Chelsea Physic Garden was a place where apothecaries could study medicinal plants.

A plan of the Chelsea Physic Garden, dated 1751 (far right).

When the Society of Apothecaries received their charter from England's James I in 1617, it set up a training program for their apprentices. This included not only the treatment of disease, but the recognition and cultivation of the many healing plants that were in the apothecary's pharmacopoeia, or handbook of medicines. Students were taken on local field trips and on "simpling voyages" (collecting medicinal plants) to places as far away as Wales and the Isle of Wight. Wherever they went, they collected specimens which were brought back to London and planted in the gardens of their colleagues and masters. The plants survived, but viewing them in their widely scattered plots was a time-consuming business. The apothecaries needed one large garden that could be shared by them all.

In 1673, they persuaded Charles Cheyne, owner of the Manor of Chelsea, to rent them a plot of land with a frontage on the River Thames for £5 a year. All the plants were brought to this one spot. The garden became well established, and in 1683 the society began a scheme of exchanging seeds and plants with Leeds University. By the beginning of the 18th century, however, enthusiasm for the garden had waned and it was looking neglected.

In 1712, the Manor of Chelsea was bought by Dr. (later Sir) Hans Sloane. He had studied at the garden during his medical training and had maintained an interest in it. He granted the apothecaries a lease at the original rent provided they maintained the garden properly.

A new head gardener was appointed, greenhouses were built for the collection of plants discovered abroad, and for a time all went well. By the 19th century, however, herbal medicine was in decline; there were no apothecaries, and nobody wanted the garden. From 1887, under the protection of the Trustees of London Parochial Charities, it was used by botany students at the Royal College of Sciences, in nearby South Kensington.

The Physic Garden survived but did not flourish until 1981, when it was handed over to a new body of trustees. An appeal was launched with the aim not only of restoring the garden to its original beauty, but also to re-establish it as a center for research and education. By 1987, sufficient funds had been raised, and in 1993 the garden was opened to the public for the first time.

The Chelsea Physic Garden is now better cared for and more informative than it has ever been. Its principal feature is the "medicinal walk." This begins at the informal beds containing the herbs that were there in Sir Hans Sloane's day, together with some dye plants and unusual vegetables. Then come the greenhouses, where visitors walk through a tropical rainforest atmosphere, home to plants such as pepper, ginger, and turmeric, and herbs used by Australian aborigines and by Zulu warriors. Outside once more, you pass the perfumery and aromatherapy border and a bed of poisonous plants. There is a plot that illustrates the history of herbal medicine, and another portraying systems of herbal healing the world over. Elsewhere there are walks shaded by ancient trees and beds depicting plant families and the history of the garden itself.

The garden is once again an important place for herbal research. Bodies such as the English Gardening School, the botany department of the Natural History Museum, and a commercial pharmaceutical company carry out projects there and contribute to the garden's income. With the growing interest in herbal cures, the Chelsea Physic Garden seems destined to thrive.

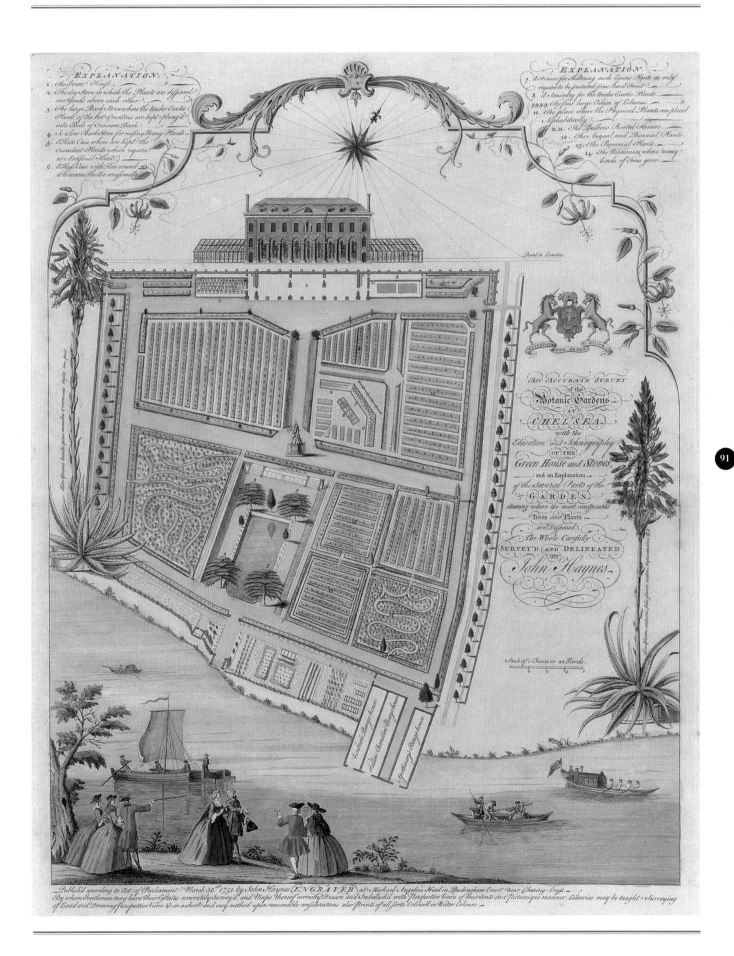

91

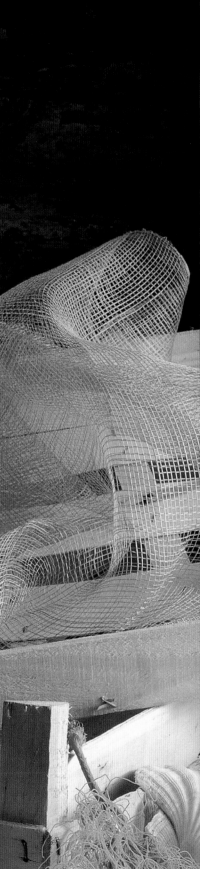

CHAPTER FOUR

FISH AND
SHELLFISH

arefully chosen herbs complement
the subtle flavors of fish and
shellfish, and their color also brightens
the appearance of many fish dishes.
From traditional parsley to exotic Thai
basil, herbs enhance sauces, marinades,
and savory butters for all kinds of fish.

FISH AND SHELLFISH

Herbs taste delicious with white fish, smoked fish, oily fish, and shellfish. Parsley is the classic fish herb. Use it to liven up a Victorian-style kedgeree made with smoked haddock and rice. Mix it with chives and bread crumbs to create a crispy topping for cod, or with lemon zest crumbs to form a coating for flounder. Stirred with chives and capers into mayonnaise, it is an ideal fish accompaniment.

Chives beaten into unsalted butter also make a rich addition to skate wings baked in lemon juice. Pungent fresh cilantro, together with ginger and green onions, gives an Eastern flavor to halibut steaks; and Thai basil leaves, chilies, lime juice, and coconut milk combine to produce a spicy shrimp dish.

Herbs that first grew on the shores of the Mediterranean are all ideal with fish. Sprigs of thyme and rosemary, tied with bay leaves, and placed inside trout before broiling, impart a subtle flavor. Make a marinade for monkfish with thyme, oregano, oil, and lemon juice; serve red mullet in a red wine sauce flavored with thyme and fennel seeds; or toss oregano into a dish of pasta and seafood. Sorrel, with its fresh, acidic leaves, goes superbly well with oily fish, particularly salmon.

Marchande et Vendeur de Poissons, *W. van Mieris, 1713.*

95

COD *with* MIXED HERB CRUST

Choose plump, square fillets from the middle of the fish for this dish, rather than pieces from the tail end. To upgrade this to dinner-party status, simply add the herb and caper mayonnaise on page 108. Serve accompanied by new potatoes and a green salad or vegetables.

SERVES 4

*1 cup fresh whole-wheat bread
   crumbs*
4 x 6oz cod fillets
*4tsp bottled black-olive
   tapenade*
3tbsp minced fresh parsley

3tbsp snipped fresh chives
4tbsp minced fresh dill
2tbsp butter, cubed
*Salt and freshly ground black
   pepper*

Preheat the oven to 400°F. Spread the bread crumbs out on a baking sheet and toast them in the oven for about 5 minutes, stirring occasionally so they do not burn. Spread the top of each cod fillet with a teaspoon of tapenade and set aside while you make the herb crust.

Combine the bread crumbs with the herbs and season well. Place a quarter of the mixture on top of each cod fillet, pressing down quite firmly. Transfer the fish to a greased baking dish and dot each with pieces of butter.

Bake for 15 minutes, until the fillets are tender and flake easily and the crust is golden brown.

Salmon *with* Sorrel Sauce

Sorrel has a slightly sharp, lemony flavor that combines very well with fish. Salmon with sorrel sauce is a classic French recipe and makes a sophisticated dinner-party dish, accompanied by new potatoes and green vegetables.

SERVES 4

4 salmon fillets	SAUCE
4oz sorrel, stems removed and leaves shredded	*4tbsp butter*
	4 shallots, minced
Generous 1½ cups shredded spinach leaves	*1 garlic clove, finely chopped*
⅔ cup light cream	*2 cups dry white wine*
1tsp Dijon mustard	*3 sprigs fresh parsley*
Salt and freshly ground black pepper	*3 sprigs fresh tarragon*
	1 sprig fresh thyme

First make the sauce. Melt 2 tablespoons of the butter in a saucepan and gently sauté the shallots for 4 minutes, until softened. Add the garlic and sauté for 1 minute longer. Pour in the wine and add the parsley, tarragon, and thyme. Bring to a boil and then leave to simmer until the sauce is syrupy and has reduced by about half.

Remove the pan from the heat and strain the liquid into a pitcher, pushing on the shallots and herbs to extract all the juice. There should be about ⅔ cup liquid: if there is less, make it up with vegetable stock; if there is more, use all of it. Discard the shallots and herbs left in the strainer.

In a separate pan, melt the remaining butter. Add the sorrel and spinach leaves and simmer for about 3 minutes, until the leaves have wilted. Add the white-wine syrup to the pan, stir in the cream and mustard, and check the seasoning. Bring to a boil and simmer for a couple of minutes. Place the sauce in a food processor and purée until fairly smooth. Return the sauce to a clean saucepan and heat through very gently.

Meanwhile, preheat the broiler to high and line a baking sheet or the broiler pan with foil. Season the salmon fillets with black pepper and broil for 5 minutes. Move the fillets closer to the heat and continue broiling for 2 to 3 minutes longer, until the top is crisp and golden.

Once the sauce has heated through, arrange the fillets on 4 warmed plates, and surround each with some of the sauce. Serve immediately.

SKATE *with* BUTTER *and* CHIVE SAUCE

This is a very light dish. Chives, with their mild onion flavor, compliment most fish, and here they are mixed with a butter that is simply melted slowly over the fish after it has been broiled. Serve with a salad or boiled potatoes and vegetables.

SERVES 4

4 skate wings, weighing 9 to 10oz each	BUTTER
½ a lemon	4tbsp unsalted butter, softened
	4tbsp snipped fresh chives
	Salt and freshly ground black pepper

To make the butter, add the chives and seasoning to the butter and beat with a wooden spoon until mixed well. Wrap the butter in plastic wrap and put it in the refrigerator to harden.

   Preheat the broiler to high. Line a baking sheet with foil and lightly brush it with oil. Arrange the skate wings on the tray, skin-side up, squeeze a little lemon juice over, and broil for 4 minutes. Turn the fish over, squeeze a little more lemon juice over, season with black pepper, and broil for 3 to 4 minutes longer. Transfer the skate to warmed plates, add a slice of the chive butter and leave it to melt slightly before serving.

SCRIMP *with* SWEET THAI BASIL

Thai basil leaves are available in Oriental supermarkets; if you cannot find them, substitute Mediterranean basil leaves, which are more common. Cilantro can also be bought from Oriental supermarkets with the roots intact; alternatively, use a tablespoon of chopped, fresh cilantro stems. Once you have made the highly aromatic paste, this dish takes just 10 minutes to cook. Serve with boiled rice.

SERVES 4

3 cilantro roots	1tsp sugar
1 garlic clove	1tsp salt
1 red chili, seeded and sliced	20 Thai sweet green basil leaves
5 black peppercorns	20 raw jumbo scrimp, defrosted if frozen, shelled
1tbsp peanut or vegetable oil	
1 cup Thai long beans or fine green beans cut in 1in pieces	2½ cups oyster mushrooms torn into bite-size pieces
1tbsp light soy sauce	
2 kaffir lime leaves or 1tbsp lime juice	
13oz can of coconut milk	
⅔ cup vegetable or fish stock	

Grind the cilantro roots, garlic, chili and peppercorns in a mortar and pestle to form a paste. Heat the oil in a frying-pan or wok over high heat, add the paste, and fry for 1 minute. Add all the other ingredients, except the jumbo scrimp and mushrooms, bring to the boil, and cover. Reduce the heat and simmer for 5 minutes. Stir in the scrimp and mushrooms and simmer for 3 minutes, until the scrimp have turned pink. Serve immediately.

John Josselyn, 17th century

John Josselyn arrived in New England in 1663, with the sole purpose to "discover all along the Natural, Physical, and Chirurgicall [Surgical] Rarities of the New-found World." Until then, little work had been done to discover and record the medicinal plants of the early colonies. The first European settlers had taken their own plants and seeds with them, but everyone knew there must be a wealth of useful native flora to be explored.
John Josselyn not only studied the plants, but he consulted and observed the Native American herbal

practitioners. The result was New England's Rarities Discovered, *published in 1672.*
The book demonstrated how people's immediate natural surroundings could supply many of their medical needs, and therefore became popular in settlers' households. Many of the remedies found their way into the American pharmacopoeia.
Unfortunately, after John Josselyn, there was little exchange of information between the settlers and the native inhabitants.

Herbs from Ancient Egypt

The ancient Egyptians were one of the first peoples to study herbs for culinary, medicinal, and aromatic uses. Herbs and spices were placed in tombs to see the soul through the afterlife and on altars as offerings to the gods. For the great and the lowly, herbs were an essential part of everyday life, and in rural Egypt today people follow the same tradition.

No Egyptian herbal has survived the centuries intact, but fragments written in hieroglyphs have come down from the 2nd century A.D. From these and from tomb evidence we know there were favorite herbs and spices. Cilantro was offered to the gods in temple ceremonies, and used in poultices for treating broken bones. Fenugreek was grown as a salad vegetable, and employed medicinally to induce childbirth and increase lactation. The seeds of black cumin (similar to the modern love-in-a-mist) were sprinkled on bread, and prescribed to treat itching skin. Cumin itself

A modern herb and spice market in Cairo, Eygpt.

❧ Basil

Basil is sowen in gardens in earthen pots . . . it is good for the hart and for the head. The seede cureth the infirmities of the hart, taketh away sorrowfulnesse which cometh of melancholies, and maketh a man merrie and glad.

GERVASE MARKHAM, 1631

was a treatment for colic and digestive disorders. Garlic, eaten daily, was a general tonic for chest ailments; and juniper was used for embalming.

Two-hundred miles into Egypt's western desert is the Kharga Oasis and near the ancient market town of Kharga, in Baqat Wells, is the recently developed Medicinal Plant Garden. Despite the fact that rainfall is almost nonexistent, this garden holds a wide variety of plants that are important to present-day Egyptian herbal and holistic medicine. There are guava trees, unknown to the pharaohs, but today providing fruit to treat upset stomachs. The flowers of hibiscus plants make a traditional tisane called *karkade*, which when sweetened with sugar acts as a restorative after long journeys. The seeds of hibiscus are reputed to be an aphrodisiac. They are also chewed to sweeten the breath and calm the nerves. Basil was known as the "royal herb" by the ancient Egyptians, and the variety grown in Baqat Wells is the spectacular aniseed basil, which can rise to 3 feet tall with a profusion of pale pink flowers.

In the town of Kharga itself, there is a herb and spice market, where local women buy herbal remedies for family illnesses, cosmetic herbs (such as henna to give their hair color and sheen), and herbs and spices for cooking. Fresh herbs are sold in bunches. The dried herbs and the spices fill bulging sacks and woven rush baskets, or are piled loosely in pyramid shapes, creating an exotic display that suffuses the air with a tantalizing aromas and transports you to the land of the pharaohs.

Eygptian female herbalists squeezing an animal skin filled with herbs. This method was used to extract the juice from herbs for use in medicinal cures.

Trout Stuffed *with* Mediterranean Herbs

Farmed trout is available all year round, making this dish ideal for a family supper. Ask your fish merchant to butterfly the fish, leaving the head and tail intact. No single herb is dominant in this recipe, which uses a combination of fresh Mediterranean herbs. Serve with new potatoes and vegetables.

SERVES 4

2tbsp olive oil
1 garlic clove, crushed
2tbsp minced fresh Italian
*   parsley*
4 trout, butterflied, with head
*   and tail on*

4 fresh thyme sprigs
4 fresh oregano stalks
4 bay leaves
4 fresh rosemary sprigs

Combine the olive oil, garlic, and parsley in a small bowl. Make 3 or 4 slashes on both sides of each fish and rub the flavored oil over the surface of each fish and into each incision. Meanwhile, divide the remaining herbs into 4 bunches (as for bouquet garnis), each bunch containing one of each herb, and tie with string. Put one bunch in the cavity of each fish and leave for 1 hour.

Preheat the broiler to medium-high. Line a baking sheet with foil and brush it with oil. Arrange the fish on the sheet and broil for 4 minutes on each side. Serve immediately, reminding your guests about the bunch of herbs in the cavity of each fish.

These fish are also delicious barbecued. Simply put each fish inside a wire fish rack or wrap each fish in oiled foil and place directly on the barbecue grid.

Monkfish Kabobs *in a* Thyme *and* Oregano Marinade

Herbs are a common ingredient in many marinades because their flavors easily infuse into the other marinade ingredients. Thyme and oregano are strong Mediterranean flavors, so place these kabobs on the barbecue and think of balmy summer days by the sea. Serve with salad or boiled rice and vegetables.

SERVES 4

1½lb skinless, boneless
*   monkfish tails*
12 large, fresh bay leaves
16 to 24 button mushrooms

Marinade
5tbsp olive oil
2 garlic cloves, crushed
2tbsp minced thyme leaves
2tbsp minced oregano leaves
2tbsp lemon juice
Salt and freshly ground
*   black pepper*

If you are using wooden skewers (you need 8 to 12), soak them in cold water for 1 hour to prevent them burning.

Remove any remaining membrane from the monkfish using the point of a sharp knife. Cut the monkfish tails into 1-inch cubes and put them in a shallow nonreactive dish. Combine all the marinade ingredients, pour over the fish, and mix well to ensure all the fish is coated. Cover and leave for 1 hour in the refrigerator.

Preheat the broiler to high or light the barbecue coals. To make the kabobs, thread monkfish cubes alternately with button mushrooms onto each skewer, wrapping a bay leaf around one cube of monkfish on each kabob. Brush the broiler pan with oil and broil the kabobs for 4 minutes on each side, or until cooked through and the flesh flakes easily. Baste with any leftover marinade during cooking.

102

RED MULLET *with* RED WINE *and* THYME SAUCE

For this dish, red mullet fillets are required. Ask the fish merchant to fillet the fish and give you the head and bones for making the sauce with. Fresh, sweet-smelling thyme is ideal for the rich, red wine sauce. A potato gratin or sauté potatoes with vegetables is the ideal accompaniment.

SERVES 4

3 tbsp olive oil	1 bay leaf
4 medium to large red mullet, filleted, head and bones reserved	Small bunch of fresh thyme
	2 tbsp fennel seeds
3 garlic cloves, quartered	2½ cups full-bodied red wine
1 leek, sliced	⅔ cup vegetable stock
2 shallots, roughly chopped	Salt and freshly ground black pepper
1 carrot, sliced	

Heat 2 tablespoons of the oil in a saucepan and gently fry the fish head and bones for 3 to 4 minutes. Stir in the garlic, leek, shallots, carrot, bay leaf, thyme, and fennel seeds and cook for 5 minutes longer. Pour in the red wine and stock, season well, and bring to a boil. Reduce the heat and simmer, covered, for 25 minutes.

Remove the lid and simmer for 5 minutes longer, to reduce the sauce. Strain the sauce into a small pan, cover, and keep over a very low heat while pan-frying the fish.

Heat the remaining 1 tablespoon of oil in a skillet and gently fry the red mullet fillets for 3 to 4 minutes on each side. Transfer the fish to warmed serving plates and serve immediately, accompanied by the sauce.

104

Samuel Hahnemann, 1755–1843

Samuel Christian Friedrich Hahnemann.

Samuel Hahnemann was the founder of homeopathy. He was a German physician, qualified in conventional medicine, who was also an experimental chemist. He was disillusioned with the bleeding, blistering, and mercury treatments of orthodox medical practice and certain he could find a more effective alternative. During experiments with the plant cinchona, used as a cure for malaria, he found that if it was taken by a healthy person it produced malarialike symptoms. These symptoms, he discovered, stimulated the body's natural immune system.

With a few pupils, he began experimenting with other plant cures and soon determined the smaller the dose, the more effective it was. This became the basis for homeopathy. Samuel Hahnemann developed 95 remedies, mostly plant-based, but some of mineral or animal extractions.

Regular doctors despised his work but, by 1813, homeopathy had become very popular in Germany and was beginning to spread to other parts of Europe.

Hans B. Gram, a Danish medical student in the United States, heard about homeopathy on a trip to Copenhagen. In 1825 he opened America's first homeopathic practice, in New York City.

STEAMED HALIBUT *with* CILANTRO

Steaming is a healthy way of cooking fish because it doesn't use added fat and the fish retains most of its vitamins and minerals. Cilantro is an intensely fragrant herb and, as the fish steams, it picks up the herb's aroma. Cilantro is used in many cuisines, including Thai, Chinese, Indian, Turkish, Portuguese, and North African, as well as Tex-Mex dishes. Serve accompanied by boiled rice and stir-fried vegetables.

SERVES 4

4 halibut fillets or steaks
Large bunch of fresh cilantro
*   (about 2oz)*
4 green onions, thickly sliced
1-inch piece of fresh gingerroot,
*   peeled and thinly sliced*

To GARNISH
Fresh cilantro sprigs
2 green onions, sliced
*   diagonally*

To SERVE
2tbsp soy sauce (optional)

Make 2 or 3 slashes across both sides of each halibut fillet or steak. Line the bottom of a steamer with half the cilantro and a few of the slices of green onion and ginger. Put the fish on top and cover with more green onions, ginger, and the remaining cilantro. (If there is not room in the steamer to put the fish in a single layer, use a double-tiered steamer or steam them in 2 batches, keeping the cooked fish warm.) Cover the steamer and put it over a pan of simmering water. Steam the fish for 10 minutes, until it is tender and the flesh flakes easily. As a rough guide, cook the fish for 10 minutes for 1-inch of its thickness; measure the fish at its thickest part and calculate the cooking time from this.

Remove and discard the cilantro, green onions, and ginger and transfer the halibut to a warmed serving dish. Garnish with sprigs of cilantro and slices of green onion and put the soy sauce in a small bowl for dipping the fish into, if you wish. Serve immediately.

105

The Herb Garden, Cloisters Museum, New York City

Hop on a bus on New York's Madison Avenue, travel for about an hour past Columbia University and Washington Heights and through Spanish Harlem and, on the very northern tip of Manhattan, you reach a hilltop outside beautiful Fort Tryon Park. Within a few minutes you can be transported into medieval Europe.

The Cloisters Museum, donated by John D. Rockefeller Jnr., belongs to the Metropolitan Museum of Art in New York. Although it was constructed in the 20th century, it incorporates parts of five original medieval cloisters and is distinctly medieval in appearance. It was built to serve as an appropriate backdrop for medieval works of art which may have seemed out of place in a modern building in central New York City.

Best known of the Cloisters Museum exhibits are the beautiful unicorn tapestries, which were woven in Brussels at the beginning of the 16th century and show seven scenes telling the story of the hunt of the unicorn. The backgrounds of all the principal pictures of these tapestries are scattered with embroidered flowers, some known and others fanciful. The museum, surrounded by herb gardens, is an apt setting.

Outside, the grounds are divided into three main cloister gardens: the Trie, the Cuxa Cloister Garth, and the Bonnefont. They are all places of interest and tranquillity, and all quite different. Go straight from the unicorn tapestries to the Trie cloister garden and you will find the images come to life, for this garden contains all the recognized plants from the tapestries. The Cuxa Cloister Garth garden, inside an enclosed courtyard, is bordered with beds of medieval and modern herbs. Around the central fountain are well-kept lawns crossed by a pattern of paths. In winter, the open walkways are covered over by glass, providing an ideal environment for pots of aloe, bay, citrus trees, acanthus, jasmine, and rosemary.

Step inside the Bonnefont cloister garden and you return to the peace of a medieval monastery. Although the design is not based on any specific monastery garden, it has all the typical features of such a place. It is enclosed by a wattle fence, and there are raised beds and a central well surrounded by four quince trees. It contains 250 species of plants that are known to have been grown in monastery gardens throughout the entire medieval period. It is a place for enjoyment and for quiet reflection.

After exploring the gardens you can sit on the terrace, surrounded by pots of fragrant trees, and enjoy the views of Fort Tryon Park, the Hudson River, George Washington Bridge, and the state of New Jersey.

To leave off the properties of Simples, we come now to the conveniences of a Garden, which are manifold in respect of Speculation, by which I mean mere walking, or at most, but gathering such things as please them, which I count no labour, for that I intend to oppose as the practicall use. That there is no place more pleasant, may appear from God himselfe, who after he made Man, planted the Garden of Eden.

WILLIAM COLES, *ART OF SIMPLING*, 1657

A courtyard herb garden at the Cloisters Museum. The garden contains a variety of both medieval and modern herbs (far right).

CRUMBED FLOUNDER *with* HERB *and* CAPER MAYONNAISE

A combination of herbs and capers is known as *salsa verde* or *sauce verte*, meaning "green sauce" in Italian and French respectively. Here, the sauce has been added to mayonnaise and makes a great accompaniment to the lightly crumbed and fried flounder fillets.

SERVES 4

⅔ cup milk
¾ cup very fine white bread crumbs, made from 1 to 2 day-old bread
1tsp grated lemon zest
2tbsp minced fresh parsley
8 flounder fillets, skinned
3 to 4tbsp vegetable oil

MAYONNAISE
3tbsp minced fresh flat-leaved parsley
1tbsp snipped fresh chives
2tbsp capers, minced
1tsp wholegrain mustard
1tbsp lemon juice
6tbsp mayonnaise
Pinch of salt and white pepper

First make the mayonnaise. Combine all the ingredients in a small bowl and mix well. It should resemble a coarse paste; if it is too lumpy, blend in a food processor or mortar and pestle for a few seconds, to break down any lumps. Set aside, to let the flavors develop, while you prepare the fish.

Season the milk with salt and pepper and mix the bread crumbs with the lemon zest, parsley, and seasoning. Dip each piece of fish in the milk and then into the bread crumbs, coating each piece well.

Heat half the oil in a large skillet and shallow fry half the fillets for 2 minutes on each side, until golden. Drain them on paper towels, then fry the remaining fillets. Serve immediately, with the herb and caper mayonnaise.

108

KEDGEREE

In England and Scotland, in the Victorian era, kedgeree was often one of many dishes laid out on a groaning sideboard for breakfast. Nowadays, it is more likely to be eaten at brunch, lunch, or as a late supper. Although kedgeree is a meal in itself, it can also be accompanied by a salad or some vegetables. The parsley stirred through during the final stages of cooking really livens up the dish.

SERVES 4

1lb smoked haddock fillets	*2tsp hot curry powder*
5 black peppercorns	*1¼ cups long-grain white rice*
1 bay leaf	*Juice of ½ lemon*
3 eggs	*3tbsp chopped parsley*
6tbsp butter	*Salt and freshly ground black*
1 onion, minced	*pepper*

Put the eggs in a pan of cold water, bring to a boil, and then leave to simmer for 10 minutes. Drain the eggs and cool them under cold water.

Meanwhile, poach the smoked haddock fillets in 2½ cups lukewarm water in a saucepan. Place over medium heat and bring gently to a boil, then reduce the heat and leave to simmer for 5 minutes. Remove the haddock fillets and keep them warm.

Strain the poaching liquid into a pitcher. Put the rice in a strainer and rinse it thoroughly under cold running water.

Melt half the butter and gently sauté the onion with the curry powder for 10 minutes, until softened. Stir in the rice and ensure the rice is coated with the onions and spices. Make up the poaching liquid, using water, to twice the volume of the rice, pour it over the rice, and stir briefly. Bring to a boil, then reduce the heat. Cover with a tightly fitting lid and leave to simmer for 15 to 20 minutes, until the rice is tender and the liquid has been absorbed. (If the liquid is absorbed too quickly, add additional water.)

Meanwhile, remove the skin from the fish and flake the flesh into large chunks. Peel the eggs and chop them. Once the rice is tender, stir in the fish, eggs, lemon juice, chopped parsley, and seasoning. Stir carefully, then cover and cook over very low heat for 5 minutes longer.

Stir in the remaining butter and serve immediately.

SEAFOOD PASTA *with* OREGANO

White fish fillets, shrimp, and squid combine with tomato and oregano to make a delicious pasta sauce. This dish should be served as soon as possible after cooking, otherwise the squid and shrimp may become tough and chewy.

SERVES 4

10oz tagliatelle	*10oz flounder fillet, skinned*
2tbsp olive oil	*and cut into 1-inch cubes*
1 onion, chopped	*4oz raw jumbo shrimp, shelled*
2 garlic cloves, crushed	*and defrosted if frozen*
1tsp chili flakes	*2 small squid tubes, cut into*
1¼lb canned crushed tomatoes	*rings (optional)*
3tbsp finely chopped fresh	*1 cup Greek wrinkled-skin*
oregano	*black olives*
Salt and freshly ground black	*Fresh oregano leaves, to*
pepper	*garnish*
10oz cod fillet, skinned and cut	
into 1-inch cubes	

Cook the tagliatelle in a large pot of boiling water for 10 to 12 minutes, or until *al dente*. Drain and transfer the pasta to a warmed serving dish to keep warm.

Meanwhile, heat the oil in a skillet. Add the onions, and fry gently for about 10 minutes, until softened but not browned. Add the garlic and chili flakes and fry for 1 minute longer. Stir in the tomatoes, oregano, and seasoning, bring to a boil and then leave to simmer, uncovered, for about 15 minutes. Add the cod and flounder and leave to simmer for 2 minutes longer. Stir in the shrimp, squid rings, and olives, and simmer for a final 2 minutes.

Check the seasoning and put a couple of spoonfuls of the sauce into the pasta and toss well. Pour the remaining sauce over the pasta, garnish with oregano leaves, and serve immediately, accompanied by a mixed salad and bread.

CHAPTER FIVE

SAUCES, RELISHES, AND DIPS

Herbs add savor to all the best dishes. Spice up a meal with a herb-flavored sauce; accompany a main dish with a relish; make a herb-flavored dip for crispy vegetable sticks; or toss a fresh green salad in a herb dressing.

Sauces, Relishes, and Dips

Herb-flavored sauces, relishes, dressings, and dips all help to make meals exciting and appetizing. Sauces can be based on a variety of ingredients. Tomato sauces can take on many guises, depending on the herbs and other flavorings used. With bay leaves and oregano, tomatoes make a sauce for pasta; and with cilantro and chilies, they become a Mexican salsa. The combination of tomatoes, cilantro, coconut, chilies, sugar, and vinegar, simmered together until syrupy, gives a relish with a distinctly Oriental flavor.

Red bell peppers can be roasted and puréed to make a sauce base that is particularly delicious when flavored with rosemary. The combination of pine nuts, olive oil, Parmesan cheese, and basil produces pesto, a classic Italian pasta accompaniment. Sour cream makes a creamy sauce base. Flavor it with dill and you have a wonderful companion for fish.

Dill and yogurt combine to make a simple cheese, known in the Middle East as labna; and a mixture of garden herbs with cream cheese provides a quick-and-easy dip. A classic French dressing or a well-made mayonnaise will always turn a selection of raw vegetables into a delectable salad. Flavor it with a blend of fresh herbs that complements the other constituents of the meal.

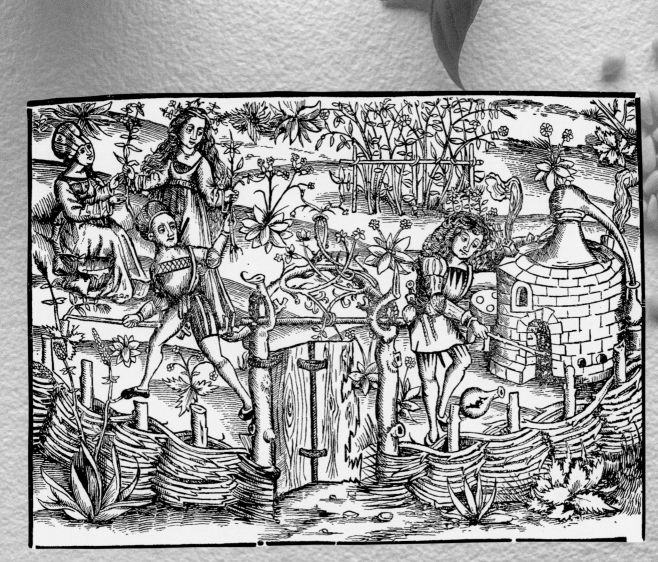

Flowers and herbs in a distillery garden, German manuscript, 1521.

113

Coconut *and* Cilantro Relish

Sweet relishes make ideal accompaniments to spicy foods and cold platters. Grated fresh coconut is occasionally found in Oriental supermarkets. If none is available, crack open a coconut, peel off the brown skin, and grate the white flesh yourself.

MAKES ABOUT 1 POUND

*3 cups peeled, seeded, and
    roughly chopped tomatoes*
*1¼ cups grated fresh coconut
    (or grate the flesh of 1
    coconut, weighing 10 to
    12oz)*

¾ cup sugar
½ cup white vinegar
¼tsp cayenne pepper
½tsp salt
*4tbsp roughly chopped fresh
    cilantro leaves*

Put the tomatoes, coconut, sugar, vinegar, cayenne pepper, and salt in a saucepan with ⅔ cup water and simmer over low to medium heat, covered, for about 50 minutes, until the mixture becomes syrupy. Remove the relish from the heat and allow it to cool. Stir in the cilantro.

If you are making this to keep, once the relish has cooled, transfer it to sterilized jars and seal. Store in the refrigerator. Use within a month of making.

ROASTED RED PEPPER *and* ROSEMARY SAUCE

This sweet sauce is a good accompaniment to fish, meat, poultry, and vegetables. You can make it in advance and then reheat it. If you do this, do not remove the rosemary until the sauce is reheated, to let a deep flavor develop.

MAKES ABOUT 1¼ CUPS

4 large red bell peppers
4tbsp olive oil
4 fresh rosemary sprigs
1 to 1¼ cups vegetable stock

1tsp lemon juice
Salt and freshly ground black pepper

Preheat the oven to 375°F. Halve each pepper and remove the white pith and seeds. Put the pepper halves on a foil-lined baking sheet or in a baking dish, pour the oil over and add a few broken sprigs of rosemary. Roast the peppers in the oven for 30 minutes.

Once the peppers have roasted, push them into the middle of the tray, and cover them with a glass bowl. Leave to cool for about 10 minutes, then peel. Put the peppers in a food processor, along with any cooking juices or oil, and purée until smooth. Transfer the purée to a saucepan, add the remaining rosemary, the lemon juice, and sufficient vegetable stock to make a pouring consistency and simmer gently for about 10 minutes. Check the seasoning. The sauce is now ready to serve.

CREAMY DILL SAUCE *for* FISH

This sauce is particularly suitable for fish dishes and is very quick and easy to make.

MAKES ABOUT 1 CUP

1tbsp olive oil
2 small shallots or 1 small onion, minced
1 cup sour cream or crème fraîche

1tsp lemon juice
2tbsp chopped fresh dill
Salt and freshly ground black pepper

Heat the oil in a small saucepan over medium heat and gently sauté the shallots or onion for about 5 minutes, until softened. Stir in the sour cream or crème fraîche and lemon juice and stir to melt. Simmer for 1 minute, then stir in the dill. Season and serve immediately.

Maud Grieve, 1858–1929

Mrs. Grieve, as she was known by the time of her death, was born in London, and when she was first married, traveled extensively in India.

On their return to England, they settled at a house called The Whins, in Buckinghamshire, and set about growing a wide range of herbs. By 1914, The Whins was known as "Whin's Vegetable Drug Plant Farm and Medical Herb Nursery," and Mrs. Grieve had acquired a great knowledge of her subject.

At the beginning of World War I, the British government advocated the growing of medicinal herbs to replace those that had previously been imported. Many people with small plots of land became enthusiastic growers, and Mrs. Grieve began writing pamphlets and running courses at home on all aspects of cultivating and using herbs. She did a good deal to revive the herb industry in England, only for it to suffer a slump after the war when cheap imports returned.

Mrs. Grieve had intended to collect all her pamphlets into a book, but she died before this could be done. Her vast store of information was collated by Mrs. C. F. Leyel and finally published in 1931. Although slightly outdated, it is one of the most comprehensive books on herbs ever written, containing details of the botanical, medicinal, culinary, historical, and mythical aspects of herbs. It continues to be widely read by herb lovers.

115

CILANTRO SALSA

Salsa is a traditional tomato sauce frequently eaten with Mexican and Tex-Mex food; it's hot and spicy, just like the type of Latin American big-band dance music that shares its name. Many different recipes exist for making salsa, with some using just raw ingredients and others cooked. This is a cooked salsa that has been tried and tested over several years. Serve as an accompaniment to tortilla chips, fried meats and poultry, and all Mexican dishes.

MAKES ABOUT 1 CUP

1 cup canned crushed tomatoes
3 small shallots or 1 small
   onion, roughly chopped
1 fresh red chili, seeded and
   minced
4tbsp roughly chopped fresh
   cilantro leaves

Put all the ingredients in a food processor and process for about 10 seconds, so the salsa still has a little texture. Transfer to a small saucepan and bring to a boil. Reduce the heat and simmer for 5 minutes, then let cool.

FRESH BASIL PESTO

Fresh pesto is delicious served with a piping-hot bowl of pasta. Making pesto the traditional way using a mortar and pestle gently squeezes and tears the basil leaves, imparting a delicious, full flavor. Keep for up to a month in the refrigerator; simply store it in a jar, covered with a thin layer of oil.

SERVES 4

1tbsp pine nuts
1½oz Parmesan cheese, roughly crumbled
1 fat garlic clove, quartered
5tbsp extra-virgin olive oil
25 fresh basil leaves, roughly torn

To Garnish
Freshly grated Parmesan cheese
Salt and freshly ground black pepper

Fresh pesto can be made slowly, with a mortar and pestle in the traditional way, or quickly, using a food processor in the modern way. If a mortar and pestle are available, use these to purée all the ingredients gradually together; it takes 25 to 30 minutes to form a delicious, aromatic paste.

Alternatively, put all the ingredients in a food processor and blend for a couple of seconds. The texture can vary from quite rough to very smooth, depending on your choice.

To serve, put a spoonful of pesto in the middle of each guest's dish of hot pasta and invite them to toss the sauce through the pasta. Offer additional freshly grated Parmesan cheese and salt and black pepper.

Herbs for Bees and Butterflies

One of the most pleasurable experiences of the summer is to sit on a warm, sunny day and watch the bees and butterflies hovering over a garden of fragrant herbs.

A herb garden can provide all that bees and butterflies need. The bees come for pollen to make honey, while the butterflies are seeking food, a place to lay their eggs and, eventually, somewhere to hibernate.

In the times when bee skeps (hives made from straw) were used, beekeepers rubbed the inside of new skeps with herbs such as mint, balm, sweet cicely, or wild thyme in the belief that a swarm would be attracted to the sweet scents. They also made sure that the same fragrant plants grew in profusion nearby.

The natural oils of the plants from which the bees gather the pollen affect the flavor of the honey, so plants were chosen to give the preferred flavor. Wild thyme seems to have been the favorite. The poet Spenser called it "bee-

Bees love fragrant herb flowers. Plants such as balm growing near a hive encourage them to stay.

An arch of honeysuckle above a bed of herbs will always attract bees and butterflies to the garden.

A walled garden creates a still, warm atmosphere where bees and butterflies can collect pollen undisturbed.

What was Paradise, but a Garden and Orchard of trees and hearbes full of pleasure? and nothing there but delights?

WILLIAM LAWSON, 1617

Formal knot gardens were popular in Tudor times, especially with beekeepers. They provided pollen-rich flowers for the bees and were a delight to look at.

alluring thyme." Thomas Hyll, in his *Gardener's Labyrinth* of 1577, said: "The owners of hives have a perfite forsight and knowledge what the increase or yields of honey will be every year by the plentiful of small number of flowers growing and appearing on the thyme about the Summer solstice. For this increaseth and yeeldeth most friendly flowers for the bees, which render a colour and savour to the Honey."

Butterflies come into the garden from midsummer to early fall. They feed in the sun on nectar-rich blue flowers and lay their eggs on suitable large leaves. They hibernate in the fall, and herbs that have not been trimmed back could provide a suitable resting place.

PLANTING A BEE AND BUTTERFLY GARDEN

Neither bees nor butterflies like to be cold or to be buffeted by winds, so choose a sheltered, south-facing corner of the garden with a wall or fence behind it. A nearby shed or greenhouse will provide space for butterflies to hibernate, and a patch of nettles somewhere close will be an ideal place for them to lay their eggs.

Many of the herbs that are grown for culinary and aromatic purposes are loved by bees and butterflies. These include rosemary, lavender,

bergamot (sometimes called bee balm), balm (its Latin name *Melissa* was an old country name for a bee), basil, marjoram (particularly the variety known as golden marjoram), hyssop, savory, thyme, sage, woodruff, viper's bugloss, and catmint (*Nepeta mussinii*).

Bees also love borage, clary sage, red clover, meadowsweet, poppy, nasturtium, mullein, and wallflowers.

"The Husbandman preserves it most in his Bee-garden," said Gervase Markham in the 16th century of the wallflower, "for it is wondrous sweet and affordeth much honey."

Butterflies love most of all the flowers of the buddleia bush, and this can be grown at the back of your bee and butterfly plot. They are also attracted to lilac, globe thistles, evening primroses, Michaelmas daisies, periwinkles, and the ice plant (*Sedum spectabile*).

FRESH HERB MAYONNAISE

Making homemade mayonnaise is a very satisfying experience and the end result is delicious. To make a herb mayonnaise, simply stir in fresh herbs to the thick, creamy sauce. Practically any herb can be used, although the more "woody" ones, such as rosemary and thyme, are less suitable. The cheat's method of making herb mayonnaise is simply to stir a few tablespoons of chopped fresh herbs into commercial mayonnaise and leave it to stand for 30 minutes to 1 hour to let the flavors develop. Homemade mayonnaise will keep for up to a week in the refrigerator.

MAKES ABOUT 1¼ CUPS

2 large egg yolks*
1 tsp Dijon mustard
1¼ cups vegetable or olive oil
1 tbsp lemon juice

Pinch of ground white pepper
2 tbsp minced fresh herbs (such as basil, tarragon, chives, chervil, parsley, and/or cilantro)

Ensure all the ingredients are at room temperature. Put the egg yolks and mustard in a bowl and beat together. Next, with a hand-held electric mixer or food processor in motion, start to add the oil *very* slowly, starting with a single drop at a time and blending the mixture well before adding more oil. Always keep the mixer in motion and continue to add the oil drop by drop, until the mayonnaise starts to thicken. Once it starts to thicken, the oil can be added in larger drops but always make sure that you have incorporated all the oil before adding any more. Once you have added half the oil, add the rest in a steady stream. Continue blending until all the oil is used up and the mayonnaise is thick and creamy. Then stir in your choice of herbs, the lemon juice, and pepper. For a deeper flavor, allow the mayonnaise to stand for 30 minutes to 1 hour before serving.

Do not be tempted to add the oil faster than a drop at a time at the beginning or the mixture will curdle and will not thicken. If the mayonnaise starts to curdle at any time, beat in 1 to 2 teaspoons boiling water. If this fails, put another egg yolk in a clean bowl, very slowly add the curdled mixture one drop at a time, and then continue as above.

*NOTE: Some eggs have been shown to contain salmonella so the elderly, young, babies, pregnant women, and people with poor immune defense systems are advised not to eat raw or lightly cooked eggs.

FRESH HERB SALAD DRESSING

Liven up a bowl of salad leaves simply by adding a wonderful herb dressing. The dressing will keep for four to five days, but after that the herbs may start to deteriorate in flavor. Almost any herbs are suitable but, in particular, try basil dressing over a tomato and mozzarella salad, tarragon dressing over a chicken salad, or dill dressing over a seafood salad.

SERVES 4

6 tbsp extra-virgin olive oil
2 tbsp white-wine vinegar
½ tsp mustard powder

1 to 2 tbsp minced fresh herbs
Salt and freshly ground black pepper

Combine all the ingredients in a screw-top jar and shake well. Just before serving the salad, pour half the dressing over and toss well.

Store the remaining dressing in a cool, dark place, out of direct sunlight.

TWO MINT SAUCES

Mint is used in sauces all over the world; in Britain, for example, mint sauce is ubiquitous with roast lamb, and in India *raita* is frequently served with spicy curries to cool the palate.

TRADITIONAL MINT SAUCE FOR
ROAST LAMB
1 tbsp sugar
1 tbsp boiling water

2 to 3 tbsp chopped fresh mint
3 tbsp white-wine vinegar

Dissolve the sugar in the boiling water in a small bowl. Add the remaining ingredients and leave for at least 1 hour before serving to let the flavors develop.

RAITA
½ small cucumber, peeled and grated
1¼ cups plain yogurt

2 tbsp minced fresh mint
Salt and white pepper

Put the cucumber in a strainer, sprinkle it with salt, and leave to drain for 15 minutes. Rinse the cucumber and squeeze out most of the juice. Put the yogurt in a bowl and stir in the cucumber, mint, and seasoning. Let stand for 10 to 15 minutes to let the flavors develop.

Bay Leaf *and* Oregano Sauce *for* Meat *and* Pasta

If you're looking for a variation on the usual tomato sauce for pasta and meat, try this one. It is quick to make, and can be made in advance and reheated. It is also suitable for freezing, so if there is a glut of tomatoes in the summer, make plenty and freeze it.

MAKES ABOUT 2½ CUPS

2 tbsp olive oil	8 bay leaves
1 large onion, chopped	1 tbsp minced fresh oregano
1 garlic clove, crushed	1 tbsp tomato paste
2½ cups fresh or canned tomatoes, crushed	Salt and freshly ground black pepper

Heat the oil in a large saucepan over medium heat and gently fry the onion for 8 to 10 minutes, until softened but not browned. Stir in the garlic and fry for 2 minutes longer. Add the remaining ingredients and simmer, uncovered, for 15 to 20 minutes longer, stirring occasionally. The sauce is now ready to serve. It is an excellent accompaniment to the homemade sausages on page 84.

122

Cream Cheese *and* Herb Dip

Thinking up new ideas for dips that are quick and easy isn't always easy but here's one that can be made in just a couple of minutes. Change the herbs according to what is available in your garden or refrigerator, if you don't have the ones suggested here.

SERVES 2

Generous ¾ cup cream cheese	Pinch of salt and white pepper
1 tbsp snipped fresh chives	
1 tbsp chopped fresh parsley	To Serve
1 tbsp chopped fresh tarragon	Crudités, bread sticks,
1½ tbsp lime juice	Melba toast, or toasted pita bread

Put the cream cheese in a bowl and beat until smooth. Add the remaining ingredients and beat again until well blended. If possible, leave the dip to stand for at least 1 hour to allow the flavors to develop.

Samuel Thomson, 1769–1843

Samuel Thomson was the son of a farmer from Alstead, New Hampshire. His circumstances were poor, he was born with a club foot, and as a child he was always ill. Conventional doctors, with their mercury-based medicines and techniques of bleeding and blistering, could do little for him, but he gradually improved under the care of the Widow Benton, a local herb-doctor who lived close to his parents.

By the time he was eight years old, Samuel Thomson had himself become extremely interested in the healing abilities of plants and, guided by the Widow Benton, he set about making his own discoveries, his most valuable being the healing properties of lobelia.

He stood by as conventional medicine failed to prevent the death of his mother, but when his daughter became ill and the physicians proclaimed her near to death, he took matters into his own hands. Dismissing the doctors, he instinctively held his sick child over a hot steam bath and watched as she began to relax and grow better. After her complete recovery, he made this treatment one of the basics of Thomsonian medicine.

Convinced that his methods were far more gentle and effective than those of the doctors, he used a system of fasting, steaming, and about 65 herbal remedies first on his own family and later on his neighbors. He became famous throughout the country and successfully treated cases of yellow fever in New York in 1806.

YOGURT *and* DILL CHEESE

This type of cheese is known as *labna* in the Middle East where it is served as part of a *meze*, which is a selection of dishes served together as an hors d'oeuvre or light meal. Although the cheese has to be left to drain overnight, it is so simple to make it is well worth the wait. It can be served on its own as an appetizer or as one of a selection of dips and spreads.

Put all the ingredients into a bowl and mix well. Fold a large piece of cheesecloth in half and put it in a strainer. Pour the cheese mixture into the cloth, gather up the ends, and tie them with string. Remove the bag from the strainer and hang over a bowl to drain overnight.

MAKES ABOUT 1¾ CUPS

1¾ cups Greek yogurt, or thick plain yogurt
5tbsp minced fresh dill
1 garlic clove, crushed (optional)

Pinch of salt and white pepper

TO SERVE
Bread sticks, toasted bread, pita bread, or crusty bread

123

CRANBERRY *and* SAGE SORBET

Cranberries are synonymous with Thanksgiving and Christmas. Here, they are joined by sage leaves to make a tangy sorbet. As sage has an overpowering flavor, just enough is added to reduce the sharpness of the cranberries. Many varieties of sage can be used, such as pineapple sage and icterina sage.

SERVES 4

½ pound cranberries, thawed if frozen
2½ cups water
½ cup plus 2tbsp sugar
⅔ cup fresh orange juice, strained
30 sage leaves, roughly torn

Put the cranberries in a saucepan with half the water and bring to a boil. Once the skins have popped, stir in the sugar and simmer gently until it dissolves. Allow the mixture to cool slightly, then purée in a food processor and push through a strainer, to remove the skins and seeds. Stir in the orange juice.

Put the remaining water in a saucepan with the sage leaves, and bring to a boil. Boil hard for about 5 minutes, until the liquid has reduced by just over half. Leave to cool, squeezing the leaves with a spoon occasionally to release all the flavor. Once the liquid has cooled, stir it into the cranberry purée and transfer to a plastic container. Cover with plastic wrap and freeze until semifrozen. Uncover and stir well or whisk with an electric mixer to break up the ice crystals. Return the sorbet, covered, to the freezer until it is frozen. Alternatively, follow the manufacturer's directions for your ice cream/sorbet machine.

Remove the sorbet from the freezer 20 to 30 minutes before serving to let the sorbet to soften slightly. To serve, spoon the sorbet into stemmed glasses.

124

STRAWBERRY *and* ROSEMARY SORBET

This sorbet has a very subtle flavor of rosemary, which combines well with strawberry.

SERVES 4

½ cup water
½ cup plus 2tbsp sugar
2tbsp chopped fresh rosemary leaves (no stems)
6tbsp lemon juice
1lb strawberries, hulled
¼ cup dry white wine, chilled

TO GARNISH
Strawberries, halved
Small fresh rosemary sprigs

Put the water, sugar, rosemary, and 2 tablespoons of the lemon juice in a saucepan, bring to a boil, and simmer until the sugar dissolves. Remove from the heat and let the syrup cool. Purée the strawberries in a blender until smooth, then strain them and add the remaining lemon juice. Strain the syrup through a nylon strainer to remove the rosemary, stir into the strawberry purée, and add the chilled wine. Mix well, transfer to a plastic container. Cover with plastic wrap and freeze until semifrozen, then stir well. Return to the freezer, covered, until it is frozen.

HONEY *and* LAVENDER ICE CREAM

The fragrant, sweet scent of lavender comes from the stems and leaves, not just the flowers. Lavender can be used to infuse cream and sugar syrups, to make great flavorings for ice creams, sorbets, cakes, and soft drinks. Sweetened with honey, this ice cream tastes exactly as the flower smells.

SERVES 4

8 to 10 stems and heads of fresh lavender
¼ cup light cream
3tbsp clear honey (flavored with lavender, if available)
3tbsp superfine sugar
3 egg yolks*
Lavender flowers, to decorate

Gently rinse the lavender and pat dry with paper towels. Then place it in a saucepan, with the cream, and bring slowly to just below a boil. Remove from the heat and stir to release the lavender's aroma. Leave the cream to cool completely so it is suffused with the full flavor of the lavender.

Once the cream has cooled, place the honey and sugar in a small saucepan with 6 tablespoons of water. Bring slowly to a boil, to dissolve the sugar, and then boil for 4 minutes, without stirring. Meanwhile, beat the egg yolks until thick and frothy. Once the sugar has boiled for 4 minutes, let it cool for 30 seconds, then pour it over the egg yolks in a steady stream, whisking constantly while pouring. Continue to whisk for about 5 minutes, until the mixture is thick. Strain the cream into the mixture, discarding the lavender, and continue whisking until the mixture is frothy and has cooled.

Pour the mixture into a plastic container and place in the freezer. Once it is semifrozen, remove from the freezer and whisk once again to remove any ice crystals. Cover the container with foil or plastic wrap and freeze until the ice cream is solid. Transfer the ice cream to the refrigerator 30 minutes before serving to let it soften slightly. Serve decorated with lavender flowers.

*NOTE: It is essential to eat the ice cream within one week as it contains raw egg. Some eggs have been shown to contain salmonella so the elderly, young, babies, pregnant women, and people with poor immune defense systems are advised not to eat raw or lightly cooked eggs.

GERANIUM *and* WHITE WINE SORBET

Infusing a sugar syrup with geranium (pelargonium) leaves imparts a subtle flavor of the smell of the leaf. Be sure any leaves you use have not been sprayed with pesticides or other chemicals. Use one of the more sweetly scented types of geranium, such as Mabel Grey, Corinda, or Attar of Roses, rather than the spicier ones.

SERVES 4

15 sweet-scented geranium leaves
1 cup water
½ cup plus 2tbsp sugar
3tbsp lemon juice
1 cup dry white wine, chilled
Geranium petals, to decorate

Rinse the geranium leaves thoroughly and scrunch them in your hands to bruise them and release the flavor. Place the water, sugar, and geranium leaves in a large saucepan, bring slowly to a boil to dissolve the sugar, and then simmer gently for 5 minutes. Remove the pan from the heat and let the syrup cool for a couple of hours.

Once the syrup has cooled completely, strain it and discard the geranium leaves. Stir in the lemon juice and the chilled wine. Mix well, transfer to a plastic container, cover with plastic wrap, and place in the freezer until half frozen. Remove, uncover, and stir to break up the ice crystals. Return the sorbet to the freezer, covered with plastic wrap, until it is frozen. Alternatively, follow the maunfacturer's directions for your ice cream/sorbet machine. To serve, spoon the sorbet into stemmed glasses and decorate with geranium petals.

General Index

Italics refer to illustration captions

INDEX *of* RECIPES

CREDITS

———

Key: *a* above, *b* below, *l* left, *r* right

Corbis-Bettmann 72*a*, 101, 107; Culpeper Ltd 31*bl* & *r*; ET Archive 9*b*, 11*a*, 19*a* & *b*, 32*b*, 36*al*, 59, 72*b*, 73*b*, 77, 82*br*, 90*a*, 91; Floris of London 24*a*; Food and Wine From France Ltd 33*br*, 37*a*; Garden Matters 37*b*, 118*br*; Herb Society, London 115; Hulton Getty 104; Image Bank 9*a*, 16, 20*a*, 36*b*, 100 (Infocus International); Mansell Collection 6*a*, 17, 25, 51; Clive Nichols 12*b*, 14*a*, 28*b*, 36*ar*, 64*a*, 82*a*, 106, 119; North Wind Picture Archives 8*a* & *b*, 13*b*, 18*a*, 22*a* & *b*, 23*l*, 28*a*, 32*a*, 33*ar*, 41, 73*a*, 82*bl*, 83*a*, 113, 118*al*; Pictor 7*a*, 54*al* & *br*, 55, 65*b*; Picture Bank Photo Library 6*b*, 10*bl* & *br*, 15*b*, 18*b*, 20*b*, 31*a*, 34*b*, 83*b*; Ann Ronan at Image Select 71; Harry Smith Horticultural Photographic Collection 7*b*, 11*b*, 12*a*, 14*b*, 15*a*, 29, 33*bl*, 64*bl*, & *br*, 118*ar*; Visual Arts Library 95; Elizabeth Whiting Associates 65*a*.
While every effort has been made to acknowledge copyright holders, Quarto would like to apologise if any omissions have been made.
All other photographs are the copyright of Quarto Publishing plc.

Author's acknowledgements (KH)
I would like to thank all those who helped during the writing and testing of the recipes in this book.
Thanks to Tim, Odette, Sue, Yvette and Steve, Richard and Claire, Simon and Lisa, Tony and Tina, Ken and Hazel, Melissa and Andy
and my family for all their support and ideas. Thanks also to my editor, Cathy Marriott, and the art editor, Clare Baggaley.